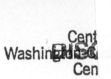
C. S. LEWIS & *MERE CHRISTIANITY*

C. S. LEWIS
& MERE CHRISTIANITY

THE CRISIS THAT CREATED A CLASSIC

PAUL McCUSKER

Tyndale House Publishers, Inc.
Carol Stream, Illinois

C. S. Lewis and Mere Christianity: *The Crisis That Created a Classic*
© 2014 Focus on the Family

ISBN: 978-1-62405-322-1

A Focus on the Family book published by
Tyndale House Publishers, Inc., Carol Stream, Illinois 60188

Focus on the Family and the accompanying logo and design are federally registered
trademarks of Focus on the Family, 8605 Explorer Drive, Colorado Springs, CO 80920.

TYNDALE and Tyndale's quill logo are registered trademarks of Tyndale House Publishers, Inc.

Scripture quotations taken from the King James Version.

Regarding the letters of C. S. Lewis: The abbreviations in quotations from letters have been
spelled out for easier reading. The author has photocopies of most of the letters referenced in
this book courtesy of the BBC Written Archives in Caversham, England. For the reader's sake,
page numbers from Walter Hooper, ed., *The Collected Letters of C. S. Lewis,* vol. 2, *Books,
Broadcasts, and the War (1931–1949)* (New York: HarperCollins, 2004), have been added.

Editor: Marianne Hering
Cover design by Stephen Vosloo
Air-raid artwork, copyright © cjp/iStockphoto. All rights reserved.
Aircraft artwork, copyright © narvikk/iStockphoto. All rights reserved.
Photograph of Lewis, copyright © Time & Life Pictures/Getty Images. All rights reserved.
Photograph of skyline, copyright © Elisabeth Pollaert Smith /Getty Images. All rights reserved.
Cover texture by Lost & Taken.

The author is represented by Books & Such Literary Agency, Janet Kobobel Grant, 52
Mission Circle, Suite 122, PMB 170, Santa Rosa, CA 95409-5370, www.booksandsuch.com.

Library of Congress Cataloging-in-Publication Data
McCusker, Paul, 1958-
 C. S. Lewis and Mere Christianity : the Crisis That Created a Classic / by Paul McCusker.
  pages cm
 "A Focus on the Family book"
 Includes bibliographical references and index.
 ISBN 978-1-62405-322-1 (alk. paper)
 1. Lewis, C. S. (Clive Staples), 1898-1963. Mere Christianity. 2. Lewis, C. S. (Clive Staples),
1898-1963—Religion. 3. Authors, English—20th century—Biography. 4. Christianity and
literature. I. Title.
 PR6023.E926Z7945 2014
 823'.912—dc23
                                        2014009524

Printed in the United States of America
1 2 3 4 5 6 7 8 9 /19 18 17 16 15 14

Contents

Prologue
1918

Jack Lewis—or Clive Staples Lewis, as he was officially known—clutched his rifle and marched across the French field of Mont Bernanchon. The ground ahead was pitted with large holes made by the cannon shells that had been falling since the campaign began. Sergeant Harry Ayres—a man Jack respected as a father figure[1]—accompanied him on the careful march across the field.

It was a spring evening and not a very pleasant one for the soldiers fighting in the Great War, as it was then called. To honor national alliances around Europe, young men of Britain and France had been drafted to repulse the German army after it invaded Belgium and marched into France. The warring sides had been fighting there for four years, mostly at an impasse, by the time Jack showed up. The only advance either side made was in the number of wounded and dead.

There were moments when the acrid smoke cleared enough for Jack to see the French village of Riez du Vinage to the northeast. At any other time it might have been a nice place to visit. Now it was merely a plot of land to be captured.

Though shells burst and gunfire sounded nearby, Jack and Sergeant Ayres stopped to consider their position. They were part of an aggressive push, their battalion moving behind a creeping barrage of shells from the British. It was unclear whether they'd advanced too far—and that was worrisome.

Jack was a five-foot–ten, heavy-set young man, only nineteen years old, and a would-be intellectual before the First Battalion of the Somerset Light Infantry enlisted him for battle. His qualifications as an officer were marginal, yet he was already a second lieutenant. He'd been fighting in the war for only a few months, having arrived the previous November. His experience thus far included digging a lot of trenches, feeling miserably cold and wet, enduring a pervasive weariness, and spending a month in the hospital with trench fever. He had also learned how to fall asleep while marching, how to wear the same boots so long that they felt as if they'd become attached to his feet, and how to ignore the stiff corpses scattered all around him.

Then the German army launched a major offensive in March. Now, in mid-April, Jack was part of the counterattack. So far the campaign was going better than expected. Many of the German soldiers gave up. At one point Jack himself had taken sixty German prisoners. But that morning the enemy regrouped for an attack from the village. The Allied forces fought back.

Explosions sounded from somewhere ahead. Men cried out and fell.

Jack looked to Ayres, the more experienced soldier. In an instant the two men realized the shells weren't coming from the Germans ahead, but from the British artillery behind them. The infantry had gained more ground than the commanders had realized. Jack and Ayres were now in the line of fire from their own cannons.

Another shell exploded.

Sergeant Harry Ayres was killed instantly by the blast. For Jack, everything went silent, and "the ground in front of [him] seemed to come up very slowly and hit [him] in the face."[2] He thought he was no longer breathing and was now facing death. "I felt no fear and certainly no courage," he later reflected. "It did not seem to be an occasion for either. The proposition 'Here is a man dying' stood before my mind as dry, as factual, as unemotional as something in a textbook. It was not even interesting."[3]

"PEACE FOR OUR TIME"

WITHIN TWENTY YEARS AFTER THE First World War—the "War to End All Wars" as it was called—the world moved toward yet another global conflict. A failed painter named Adolf Hitler rose through the political ranks in Germany by spouting an extreme nationalism that sought to reestablish Germany's preeminence among the European nations. In defiance of the peace treaties established at the end of World War I, Hitler rebuilt Germany's military might. Through the National Socialist (Nazi) Party, Hitler confounded his critics with shrewd political maneuvering, rising to the highest position of power. He became aggressive, establishing a totalitarian regime within his country and looking outward to reclaim territory Germany had lost after the last war. He demanded that the German "Aryan master race" be united, regardless of where the Aryans lived geographically. If Hitler had to invade other countries to make that happen, then he would.

The more aggressive Hitler became, the more passively the leaders in the surrounding countries seemed to respond to him. Britain's Prime Minister Neville Chamberlain was an idealist and was convinced that reason would prevail over tyranny. Certainly no one wanted a repeat of the Great War. Chamberlain believed everyone, including Hitler, truly wanted peace.

NEVILLE CHAMBERLAIN

Arthur Neville Chamberlain (1869–1940), born near Birmingham, England, was the son of a successful industrialist and progressive lord mayor of that city. As a young man he worked as a planter in the Bahamas (1890–1897); then he returned to England to pursue an industrial and political career. He was elected as a Conservative to Parliament in 1918 and, afterward, held various government positions (postmaster general, minister of health, minister of welfare). He served as the chancellor of the exchequer from 1931 until May 1937, when he succeeded Stanley Baldwin as prime minister.

Chamberlain was successful in social reform, economics, and finance, but he suffered greatly in foreign affairs because he pursued a policy of appeasement with Adolf Hitler. He endured criticism for having allowed open aggression by the dictators of Europe, yet his policies gave Britain the time it desperately needed to arm itself for war.

Thin and birdlike, Chamberlain was described by one of his adversaries as having "the mind and manner of a clothes-brush."[1] Even those close to him were often put off by his cold manner, sneering and hateful attitude, and an inherent arrogance.

Chamberlain never recovered from the circumstances that led to his downfall as prime minister. Though he hoped history might vindicate his policies, he died a melancholy and physically broken man on November 9, 1940, six months after resigning. Winston Churchill paid tribute to him in the House of Commons on November 12, 1940: "It fell to Neville Chamberlain in one of the supreme crises of the world to be contradicted by events, to be disappointed in his hopes, and to be deceived and cheated by a wicked man."[2] Then he reminded his fellow politicians that Chamberlain had placed his hope in "the most noble and benevolent instincts of the human heart—the love of peace, the toil for peace, the strife for peace, the pursuit of peace, even at great peril, and certainly to the utter disdain of popularity or clamour."[3]

Chamberlain's legacy would remain deeply ingrained in the British psyche. In 1997, author J. K. Rowling made Chamberlain the model for the character Cornelius Fudge, minister for magic, in her megahit Harry Potter book series.[4]

Only one voice—the "lone, unheeded prophet in the British land"[5]—consistently warned the British people of the dangers Hitler posed: the pudgy, round-faced, sixty-four-year-old Winston Churchill. But few wanted to hear his wisdom such as this given on October 16: "Alexander the Great remarked that the people of Asia were slaves because they had not learned to pronounce the word 'No.' Let that not be the epitaph of the English-speaking peoples, or of Parliamentary democracy, or of France, or of the many surviving liberal States of Europe."[6]

In the fall of 1938, Adolf Hitler laid claim to sections of Czechoslovakia that were filled with Germans. He stated that war was inevitable if these Germans weren't given proper autonomy. Prime Minister Chamberlain and French Prime Minister Édouard Daladier met with Hitler. Two weeks of tense negotiations followed.

The outcome was the Munich agreement, which allowed Nazi Germany to annex areas of the Czechoslovak state called the Sudetenland. The agreement was dated September 29, 1938, though it was signed in the early hours of September 30.

Prime Minister Chamberlain returned to England and, after stepping from his plane, waved the agreement victoriously to cheering crowds and announced that Britain and Germany desired never to go to war again. Later, from his official residence at 10 Downing Street, Chamberlain said the now-famous words: "I believe it is peace for our time."[7]

To this, Winston Churchill told the House of Commons:

> We have sustained a total and unmitigated defeat. . . . We are in the midst of a disaster of the first magnitude. . . . And do not suppose that this is the end. It is only the beginning.[8]

Broken Promises

No one from the democratic Czech Republic had been involved in drafting the Munich agreement—and the Czechs paid a heavy price for the so-called victory. Over the next six months, Hitler broke every term of the agreement and sliced and diced the Czechoslovak state as it suited him. By March 1939, the Nazis occupied the sections that hadn't already been taken by Hungary and Poland.

By the summer of 1939, hope for a lasting peace faded fast. The British government reluctantly mobilized its military and put stringent civil-defense measures in place throughout the country.

Government leaflets were shoved through every letter box, warning of the imminent threat of gas attacks and air raids. The catchall acronym for civil preparedness, the ARP (Air Raid Precautions), soon became as well known as the BBC (British Broadcasting Corporation). ARP handled the administration of defense plans, departments, volunteer organizations, medical services, fire, gas, lighting, air-raid protection, and "food defence." Every part of civilian life would be affected by the government. Nighttime would include "blacking-out" all windows so that no internal lighting would guide enemy aircraft to a village or city. And the absolute control of all "foodstuffs" by the government meant the rationing of the most basic supplies.[9]

ANDERSON SHELTERS

The Anderson shelter was named after the home secretary Sir John Anderson, who launched the build-your-own initiative. (The designer, William Paterson, was knighted in 1944 for his excellent, efficient, and economical shelter design.)[10] The shelter had fourteen sheets of corrugated steel bolted together to form a shell six feet high, four and a half feet wide, and six and a half feet long. It was to be buried in a backyard hole approximately four feet deep and then covered with about fifteen inches of soil. Six people could crowd into one during an air raid with reasonable safety, except for a direct hit. Most people found that the shelters smelled of earth and dampness and could be particularly uncomfortable when waterlogged, which was often.[11]

The government plan gave free Anderson shelters to lower-income families or sold them for seven pounds (over a week's wages for a working man) to families with higher incomes. More than two million shelters were assembled and were often made as cozy as possible with makeshift beds and shelves for food. More industrious people planted flowers and vegetables in the soil on top. "There was a greater danger of being hit by a vegetable marrow falling off the roof of an air-raid shelter than of being struck by a bomb," claimed one American journalist.[12]

Bomb shelters were constructed by the government beneath existing buildings. Deep trenches, covered with steel or concrete, scarred the many parks. Mandatory sandbags and fire buckets appeared in homes, hotels, and offices.

Helium-filled barrage balloons—sixty-two feet long, twenty-five feet in diameter, and attached to the ground by cables—appeared in the skies over London. Floating at five thousand feet, they would force German bombardiers to fly their planes higher, thus bombing with less accuracy.

The situation in Europe intensified. On August 23, 1939, Germany and the Soviet Union signed a non-aggression pact. On the surface it seemed like a proactive effort at peace, keeping two major powers of conflicting ideologies from fighting one another. But astute observers knew it was an act of collusion. The two countries were making peace only so they could amicably divide Poland when the time was right.

It's easy to imagine the anxiety and apprehension Jack Lewis and his entire generation felt about a return to war.

The Last Normal Day

September 1, 1939, began normally enough in Britain. It was a Friday. The weather forecast for the day and the coming weekend predicted sunshine and pleasant temperatures. Men and women went to work, hung out the laundry, saw to the children, and chatted with neighbors. Commuters walked, biked, bused, and trained into the capital city of London. It was a normal day. There was nothing to hint at how quickly everything would change for everyone.

At Broadcasting House, the BBC's formidable headquarters

in central London, the Reverend James Welch was in studio 3E.[13] Welch was the director of religious broadcasting and often spent time behind the microphone. On this occasion, at 10:15 a.m., he was leading the *Daily Service*—a fifteen-minute, live program of worship.

REVEREND JAMES WELCH

James William Welch (1900–1967) was born in Sunderland, England. At eighteen he joined the Honourable Artillery Company at the end of World War I.[14] After his stint in the army, he attended Sidney Sussex College, Cambridge, where he attained a first degree in anthropology and theology. He studied theology at Westcott House, Cambridge, and was ordained at the age of twenty-six in 1927. After joining the Church Missionary Society, he served in Nigeria for six years. He returned to England in 1935 and served as the principal of Saint John's Training College. While there he took the position of director of religious broadcasting with the BBC.

Welch was an avid follower of the archbishop of York, William Temple, who made his name preaching and writing about social reform and ecumenicalism. Welch was a staunch advocate for the League of Nations, the predecessor of the United Nations.[15]

As director of religious broadcasting, Welch was responsible for the quality of all religious material heard on the air. After listening to a series of American religious programs suggested for broadcast to the military, he declared them "appalling mush." He refused both as a BBC spokesperson and as an Anglican parson to broadcast the "pep talk" sermons, because they would be "listened to by troops in great danger."[16]

A message was passed to him: "Germany invaded Poland early this morning."[17]

Welch immediately broke the news to his listeners and then thoughtfully led them in prayer for Poland, for the people of Britain, and for trust in God.[18]

✻ ✻ ✻

Everyone tuned in to their radios—the "wireless," as everyone called it—establishing the critical role broadcasting would play in the future of the nation. The news came in bits and pieces from newsreaders who spoke in educated accents, using the King's English. The announcer betrayed no emotion as he told how German tanks, infantry, and cavalry—a total of 1.5 million troops—had penetrated Polish territory on several fronts. German planes bombed the cities. Incendiary bombs were dropped on the cities of Kraków, Katowice, Tczew, and Tunel. By 9:00 a.m., the air raids had reached Warsaw.

As the day unfolded, it became clear that there had been no warning or declaration of war from Germany, though a German radio broadcast stated that the government had presented a list of demands to Polish authorities. The Polish government officials claimed they had never received them.

Prime Minister Chamberlain met with his cabinet in the morning. In the afternoon, as a matter of protocol and duty, Chamberlain met with King George. Though the role of a monarch was mostly as a figurehead by that point in Britain's history, the king still had the authority to approve the government's plans on the mobilization of the Naval Service, British army, and Royal Air Force.

Chamberlain addressed Parliament later in the evening. The

BBC told the nation to expect a statement from Prime Minister Chamberlain.

C. S. Lewis, Shakespeare, and Poland

Jack Lewis had come a long way since being wounded in France. By 1939 he was a tutor (teaching assistant) and lecturer at Magdalen (pronounced "Maudlin") College in Oxford, a published essayist and critic, and the author of several books ranging from poetry and literary studies to science fiction and even an allegorical defense of his book *The Pilgrim's Regress: An Allegorical Apology for Christianity, Reason, and Romanticism* (1933). His reputation as an engaging lecturer led to invitations for him to give talks and present academic papers around the country.

On the day Germany invaded Poland, Jack was away from his home in Oxford to lecture in the town of William Shakespeare's birth, Stratford-upon-Avon. The town, a major tourist stop boasting Shakespeare's home and a museum and filled with theaters dedicated to performances of Shakespeare's plays, was in the final days of its annual summer-long festival dedicated to the Bard of Avon. Jack was asked to present two talks.[19]

The first lecture, delivered the day before the invasion, was titled "The Renaissance and Shakespeare: Imaginary Influences." Lewis claimed it *could* have been titled "How the Renaissance Didn't Happen and Why Shakespeare Was Not Affected by It." The lecture went well enough to be reported in the *London Times* the next day. The second lecture, about *The Taming of the Shrew*, was canceled because of the news from Europe.[20]

In all, Jack had a "pretty ghastly time," as he was stuck in a nearly empty hotel with a radio "blaring away all the time and hours and hours to get through without work." For him, it was the "worst possible background to a crisis."[21]

The only positive experience was the chance to see two Shakespearean plays—*Richard III* and *Much Ado About Nothing* ("the latter was really very good").[22]

WARREN HAMILTON LEWIS

Warren Hamilton Lewis (1895–1973), C. S. Lewis's older brother, was born in Belfast, Northern Ireland, and educated in England from the age of ten. He was tutored by W. T. Kirkpatrick (Jack's tutor later) in preparation for a place at Sandhurst Royal Military Academy. Warnie, as he was affectionately known, placed 21 out of 201 successful candidates, winning a prize cadetship to Sandhurst in 1914. His officers' training was reduced to nine months (from two years) due to the First World War in Europe. Warnie served with the British Expeditionary Force in France until the armistice of 1918. In 1921 he served in Sierra Leone, West Africa, for a year. Then he returned to England until his reassignment to China in 1927, where he commanded the supply depot in Shanghai.

In March 1930, while standing before the Great Buddha of Kamakura, Warnie converted to Christianity. He went back to England until his second tour of China in 1931, where he witnessed the Japanese attack in January 1932. He retired the following December and moved in with Jack.

A friendly, considerate, and much respected man by all who knew him, Warnie lived happily in Jack's shadow as his confidant and helper, deferring to his brother's talent and skills.

Jack returned to Oxford by train, narrowly missing Warnie at the railway station. Though Warnie had retired from active military duty in 1932, he had remained a member of the Regular Army Reserve of Officers. With the news from Poland, Warnie was sent immediately to a base in Catterick, North Yorkshire. Within two weeks he would be sent to France, where his experience in the distribution of military supplies and dealing with troop transports would become vital.

All of this was worrisome to Warnie. By this time he was forty-four, physically unfit, a heavy drinker, and, at heart, fearful of his ability to serve with the same vigor he had in the First World War. He admitted in his diary that he felt confused and frightened. Yet he was determined to do his duty.[23]

Jack knew his brother well. They had been as close as two brothers could ever be—their bonds of affection going back to childhood as playmates, surviving their mother's early death, and drawing strength from each other while living with a distant father. And while Warnie nearly idolized Jack, Jack agonized over his brother's excessive drinking. To know that Warnie might be thrown back in the thick of battle after all those years was an understandable source of anxiety. Jack wrote to Warnie immediately and regularly thereafter. "God save you, brother" he offered as a poignant closing to a letter written on September 2, 1939.[24]

Yet if Jack was worried for his brother, he was also worried for himself. He was still within the age for military enlistment—he wouldn't turn forty-one until November 29. Like Warnie, he wanted to do his duty, but he questioned his usefulness or ability to serve in the way the government might require.

He proactively met with the president of Magdalen College, George Stuart Gordon. Jack had known Gordon for years, referring to him in various letters as "Gentleman George" or "Smoothboots."[25] Gordon laughed "to scorn" Jack's worries and assured him it would all work out.[26] There was little Jack could do but hope Gordon was right.

Emergency at the BBC

The BBC was in a frenzy of activity on September 1, 1939, as its long-standing emergency war plans were quickly implemented. Sealed orders were opened at every transmitter station in the country, requiring each transmitter to synchronize with all the others on a single wavelength (rather than the variety of wavelengths the BBC had been using). This allowed the other transmitters to carry on if one transmitter were to be damaged by German bombers. Listeners would hear no more than a slight decrease in volume. Listeners were instructed throughout the day regarding which wavelength they should adjust their radios to.[27] By 8:15 that evening, listeners heard the new on-air identification for the first time: "This is the BBC Home Service."[28]

The new television service, only two years old but already broadcasting to ten thousand viewers, was suddenly unplugged. The government feared that the transmitter at the famous Alexandra Palace in London would serve as a powerful direction-finder for enemy aircraft. The last thing viewers saw was the Walt Disney cartoon *Mickey's Gala Premiere*.[29]

Many of the program departments moved away from London, as everyone was sure that the city would be the primary target of German attacks. Reverend Welch and the Religious Broadcasting department were sent to Bristol, approximately 120 miles west of London.

Amid all this internal activity, a much greater and more heart-wrenching plan was enacted for the people of London. That same evening, the BBC announced the government's instructions for evacuating the city's children.

THE KILNS AT WAR

ALMOST A MILLION YOUNG MEN from the British Empire were killed or wounded in World War I.[1] The survivors became the "Lost Generation," now older and understandably fearful of another war—and an immediate German attack. Not surprisingly, the government was motivated to do all it could to protect the next generation. Plans were implemented for the evacuation of roughly two million children from Britain's major cities.

Though the evacuations were entirely voluntary, the government exerted as much pressure as possible on reluctant parents. "Mothers—send them out of London" one poster proclaimed, with a picture of worried-looking children gazing pathetically at the camera. Another poster, anticipating the temptation to bring evacuated children back, used a drawing of a ghostlike Hitler leaning toward the ear of a mother sitting under a tree with her children and whispering, "Take them back," while the headline begged mothers, "Leave the children where they are."[2]

The majority of parents, anxious and frightened, agreed with the government's plan. Estimates vary, but approximately 1.5 million children were removed from the largest cities in England, with most from London. Some left with their mothers or fathers. Many left alone, and parents had to trust their children to strangers while they remained in the cities to work.

On paper, the plan seemed sensible. In reality, the ministries of health and transport and the board of education weren't ready for the logistical nightmare that followed. Children were taken to schools, city halls, churches, and bus and railway stations with little more than a change of undergarments, a sack lunch, and a gas mask. Some were accompanied by their heartbroken mothers. Where a parent couldn't accompany a child, one hundred thousand teachers were tasked with the job. It still wasn't enough. Only through the intervention of the Women's Royal Voluntary Service, when an additional seventeen thousand women stepped into the fray, was the traumatic process eased.[3]

The rural authorities on the receiving end were also overwhelmed. Bedding, medical supplies, water, and food were in short supply. The villagers also received a shock when they encountered the lice, scabies, rickets, and malnutrition afflicting many of the inner-city children. Some of the children had never used a proper toilet. Some had never slept in a bed. And when they did, bedwetting wasn't uncommon (a third of the children suffered from this problem). As a result, the government had to increase the laundry allowance for the host families.[4]

These physical manifestations of emotional trauma should not have been a surprise. Torn from their families, the children had to cope with deep emotional loss, if not of their mothers, then of their fathers, who had to remain back in the city, possibly to die. Adding to the trauma, not all of the villagers were willing recipients of these urban strangers. Many of the hosts resented the fact that war hadn't been officially declared or might still be avoided.[5] It was possibly a lot of unnecessary effort. Some begrudgingly took in evacuees, only to make the children's lives miserable. One woman demanded that an evacuee mother keep her small children quiet at all times. Another woman refused to allow the evacuees to use the kitchen or hang up washing to dry in the house. In a few cases, evacuee families were required to leave their hosts' houses during the day and wander the countryside until they were allowed to return in the evening.[6]

Not all of the conditions were the stuff of nightmares. Many evacuee children wound up with kind and generous families in homes with better accommodations than their city dwellings. For them, life in the countryside, as a contrast to the cities, proved blissfully quiet and almost heavenly, with green fields and fresh air.

On September 2, 1939, three anxious evacuee girls arrived at Jack Lewis's house and entered an atmosphere that would undoubtedly have been a source of blessed relief—even if an unusual one.

History of The Kilns

Though English homes are numbered, it's a quaint tradition to name one's home. The practice began in the early days of Britain's history as the wealthy named their mansions, castles, and halls. The lower classes embraced the idea, giving their homes names like Rose Cottage or Patchings or, in the case of Jack's house, The Kilns.

The Kilns was as much a description as it was a name. Built in an area called Headington Quarry, about three miles outside of Oxford, the house sat on nine acres at the base of Shotover Hill, with woods and a large pond that had once been a pit from which clay was taken for brick making. The actual kilns, which had been used to bake the bricks, still stood on the property, abandoned and covered in ivy.

OXFORD UNIVERSITY

With historical references going as far back as the eleventh century, Oxford University was true to the original idea of a university. It wasn't one large academic institution but was actually a collection of "constituent colleges"—autonomous entities with their own leadership, budgets, and academic structures.

Magdalen College was established in 1458 by the bishop of Winchester, William Waynflete. The Great Tower and the ornate, blond-colored stone[7] buildings, designed around a variety of quadrangles, were built at the end of the fifteenth century and early into the sixteenth. By the twentieth century, the college was renowned for its high quality of education in all academic fields, but particularly in literature and philosophy.

The college sat on a vast expanse of grounds on the east edge of town along the River Cherwell. There was a park where deer roamed freely. Addison's Walk, a flower-filled meadow, bordered the college and gave Jack and his fellow academics a scenic area to walk and talk. Even now it's considered one of the most beautiful colleges in the world.

Since 1925, Jack's suite of rooms[8] for tutoring—or, if necessary, sleeping—was in the New Building (built in 1733). It included a bedroom and two sitting rooms, one larger and one smaller, with windows that faced away from the city, giving Jack the impression that he'd been placed in the middle of the English countryside rather than a bustling university town. His windows overlooked a playing field for cricket, and he often gazed upon morning mist rising from the river or deer wandering over the grass and into the trees.

The ground floor of The Kilns contained two sitting rooms, two bedrooms, a kitchen and scullery, and a very small maid's bedroom. Two rooms were later added—a workroom for Jack and another for Warnie. Upstairs were another three bedrooms, though one—Jack's—could be entered only through an adjoining bedroom or an outside entrance with its own stairs.

The estate also contained a greenhouse, tennis court, garden, orchard, and a couple of small bungalows that occasionally served as storage or temporary living quarters (even though they lacked plumbing or heat).

The property had been purchased in 1930 by Jack, Warnie, and Mrs. Janie Moore and was placed legally in Mrs. Moore's name. She was, in most respects, the matriarch of The Kilns until her death in 1951.

A reasonable question for the three evacuees might have been this: Why was Jack Lewis living with a woman named Mrs. Moore?

The Moores

In 1917 Jack was a student at University College, Oxford. The First World War raged across the English Channel, and Jack was quickly enlisted to participate in the University Officer Training Corps (UOTC). Within a month he was transferred to Keble College as a cadet, with the expectation of a commission.

Jack's roommate at Keble was a young man named Paddy Moore.[9] Jack initially viewed Paddy as a "good fellow," perhaps "a little too childish," but then revised his opinion a few days later and decided he was a "very decent sort of man."[10]

Paddy's mother was Mrs. Janie Moore,[11] an Irish woman

who'd moved to Oxford with her eleven-year-old daughter, Maureen, to be close to Paddy before he was sent off to France.

ALBERT AND FLORA LEWIS

Albert James Lewis (1863–1929) was born in Cork, Ireland. In 1868, Albert's parents moved their family to Belfast for a job opportunity. Albert remained there the rest of his life. After studying law, he became a solicitor in June 1885. He fell in love with the daughter of his parish priest, Florence "Flora" Hamilton (1862–1908) and married her in 1894. The next year Warnie Lewis was born, with Jack arriving in 1898. Albert was politically and civically minded, serving on many boards and local councils.

Literature was an important part of the Lewis household. Albert was an aspiring writer and had been encouraged by his school's headmaster, W. T. Kirkpatrick, who would later tutor Albert's sons, Warnie and Jack. The Lewis house was filled with books, which Warnie and Jack devoured as small children. By all accounts, their home was a happy one, until 1908 when Flora was diagnosed with cancer. An operation gave a temporary reprieve from the illness, but only for a few months. Flora died on August 23, 1908.

Understandably, the family was devastated. Though Albert did his best to be a good father to his two sons, he dealt with his grief by retreating into his work. As the boys grew, conflicts and misunderstandings with their father intensified and beset them throughout their adult lives, though he generously provided most of the funding for Jack's education. Albert continued working at his law practice until his death on September 24, 1929.

With Warnie—his only sibling—serving in France and his father back in Ireland, Jack took to the Moores as a surrogate family. They certainly welcomed him into the fold. Within a month Jack wrote to his father, Albert Lewis, that he liked Mrs. Moore immensely. More than that, Jack had become infatuated with her.

Mrs. Moore was then forty-five and had been separated from her husband since 1907 after she left him in Ireland; they never divorced. For Jack to be attracted to an Irish woman who was willing to mother him wasn't surprising considering the loss of his own mother when he was nine. Jack would call her "Minto" or "mother," and she called him "Boysie."

Upon completing officer's training in September 1917, Jack became a second lieutenant in the Third Battalion of the Somerset Light Infantry. He was given a month's leave before going off to France. Instead of going straight home to his father, he spent half of the leave with Mrs. Moore in Bristol. His father was hurt by Jack's choice. Their relationship, volatile during the best of times, became strained—even more so when a series of telegram miscommunications caused Albert to miss seeing his son one last time before Jack was sent to France.

Paddy wasn't in the same battalion as Jack, winding up instead with the Rifle Brigade. Paddy began his tour of duty in France at the beginning of October 1917. At their final meeting, each young man promised to take care of the other's family if the worst happened in battle—a promise that became pivotal in Jack's life.

Wounds That Won't Heal

Jack arrived in France in mid-November 1917. His battalion was ordered to the front. He celebrated his nineteenth birthday in the trenches, where, for a long time, all was water and weariness.[12] There was little engagement with the enemy, as both sides remained in a military stalemate. The following February, Jack was hospitalized for three weeks with trench fever, an illness suffered by many soldiers during this war. He was released in time to join his battalion for Germany's final attack on the western front that spring.

Meanwhile, Paddy Moore's war experience and whereabouts became a mystery. He was last seen during a battle at Pargny, France, on March 24, 1918. Witnesses said he went to heroic efforts to fight "against infinitely superior numbers of the enemy."[13] His death was confirmed in April—but not to Mrs. Moore. She didn't learn her son's fate until the following September, in part because the information had been sent to her estranged husband in Ireland. He failed to let her know.

"They tell me he was taken a prisoner," Mrs. Moore explained to Albert Lewis in an October 1 letter. "[Then he] overthrew his guards, got back to our lines to be sent over again, was wounded in the leg, and as his man was bandaging him up, was shot through the head and killed instantaneously."[14]

The spring offensive by the German army in March continued into April. The Germans attacked the French city of Arras, where Lewis was posted. Jack's battalion then led a counterattack on Riez du Vinage. There are conflicting reports about what happened exactly. Without dispute, it was during the evening of April 15 that a shell exploded, killing Sergeant Harry Ayres and wounding Jack in three places. Jack fell to the ground with the wind knocked out of him. His face slammed into the mud, causing one eye to swell shut and giving the impression he'd also been wounded in the face. He recovered enough to drag himself back to his battalion, where stretcher bearers took him to a field hospital. Warnie, on hearing the news, borrowed a motorbike and rode fifty miles to see Jack.

Toward the end of May, Jack was relocated to a hospital in London. He wrote to his father begging him to come visit, but for unknown reasons, Albert didn't. Mrs. Moore did. Often.

Given the chance to transfer to a convalescent home, Jack requested one in Ireland but was denied. He then chose another in Bristol to be nearer to Mrs. Moore. In the ensuing months, their relationship became fixed. Mrs. Moore had a replacement for her dead son. Jack, who was by nature loyal and dutiful, took seriously his promise to Paddy and committed himself to her care.

From that point on, Jack, Mrs. Moore, Maureen, and, later, Warnie were a family. The arrangement would impact Jack's life and writing in ways he could not have imagined.

C. S. Lewis: Between Wars

Released from the military at the end of 1919, Jack spent the next four years at University College, Oxford, studying Greek and Latin literature, followed by philosophy and ancient history (all four subjects comprising a classics course called "Greats" at Oxford). Then he studied English literature. He received the "First Class" distinction, the highest academic achievement, in all of those subjects in 1920, 1922, and 1923, respectively.[15]

Jack was appointed fellow and tutor in English literature at Magdalen College, Oxford University, in 1925. He remained there well past World War II, accepting a position at Cambridge University in 1954.

Life with the Three Evacuees

Little is known about the first three evacuee girls.[16] One, according to Jack, was a "Rose Macaulay* child—pure boy in everything except anatomy and a reader of Henty,"[17] a popular writer of fiction for boys.

Mrs. Moore instantly established ground rules for the newcomers. They were expected to help around the house and garden; they would all share a single room; and they would *not* be eating at the table with the family.

Presumably Jack didn't challenge Mrs. Moore on some of the rules in order to keep the peace with her. But he often smuggled food up to the girls' room or, when possible, permitted them to sneak down to the kitchen for a bite to eat. While out for walks, he treated them to an occasional meal at the local fish-and-chip shop. They would eat quickly before arriving home.

Mrs. Moore also insisted that Jack was not to be bothered in his study. Jack himself broke this rule, inviting the girls in to listen to classical music or simply to chat. He also encouraged their learning by buying them books and discussing what they'd read. Some nights, after Mrs. Moore had gone to sleep, the girls would slip out of their bedroom window, onto the roof of Jack's study, and in through another window to talk with him.[18]

For his part, Jack observed the girls with a certain bemusement. In letters to his brother he recounted how, when war was declared, one of the girls jumped up and down with joy, while another added, "Perhaps there'll be an air raid *to-night!*"[19]

The girls were allowed to swim in the pond, but it had to be

---

* Rose Macaulay (1881–1958) was a popular English writer and something of a Christian mystic.

done in two shifts because there weren't enough bathing suits for all three girls. Watching them, Jack was amused to see them employ a stall tactic. He stood on the pond's edge "bawling 'Time to come out' and a head disappearing and then emerging ten yards further away to say 'What?', and then twenty yards further away still to say 'I can't hear what you say.'"[20]

He also noted how modern children were "poor creatures" because they were constantly bored and nagging their caretakers for things to do. He'd send the evacuees off to play tennis or mend stockings or write home, and as soon as that was done, they were back again with the same questions. "Shades of our own childhood!"[21] Jack exclaimed. He conceded that his father "had a great deal more patience than we boys thought."[22]

The revolving-door existence of the evacuees became clear rather quickly when, after only a couple of weeks, "the nicest of our evacuated girls (the Rose Macaulay one) [had] been taken away by a peripatetic lip-sticked mother who . . . changed her mind." In the girl's place came an "Austrian Jewess" (about the age of sixteen), whom the school said was "difficult."[23]

In a letter she wrote to Wheaton College historian Clyde Kilby, evacuee Patricia Heidelberger recalled her years at The Kilns as "two of the happiest of my school life." She wrote,

> My first impression of C. S. Lewis was that of a shabbily clad, rather portly gentleman, whom I took to be the gardener and told him so. He roared—boomed!—with laughter. . . . Unlike most evacuees, we were comfortable . . . and we seemed to be loved. I enjoyed the scholarly sessions in the den; I borrowed books; I learned about Tolkien and the Inklings. I think [we] were extremely fortunate, and more than a little spoiled.[24]

The evacuees in the Oxford area created problems for Jack in unexpected ways. Suddenly it was difficult to find a seat in church because "every local family, apparently [took] the view that whether they go or not, at any rate their evacuees *shall*." He took exception to being surrounded by a "writhing mass of bored urchins" who obviously had no idea what was going on or why.[25] It confirmed Jack's view that the people in what had once been considered a Christian country now knew little about the faith.

The presence of so many children during the war years deeply affected Jack. Friend and biographer George Sayer concluded that, without the presence of the evacuees, Jack may not have had the same depth of childlike insight or creative inspiration with the Narnia stories.[26]

✳ ✳ ✳

In one day Jack's world had changed. Europe seemed headed for another war. Mrs. Moore and her daughter, Maureen, now had three strangers in the house to worry over. Warnie had gone off to war, and Jack was still within the age range to follow.

Any hope of averting war now rested with Prime Minister Chamberlain. On the evening of September 1, 1939, in a packed House of Commons, he announced that two ambassadors in Berlin—the British and the French—had given German foreign minister Joachim von Ribbentrop an ultimatum: Unless the Nazis withdrew immediately from Poland, Britain and France would fulfill their promise to support the Polish people and go to war.

Von Ribbentrop promised only that he would pass the message on to Adolf Hitler.

REPORTING FOR DUTY

It was a beautiful Sunday morning, September 3, 1939, when Prime Minister Neville Chamberlain took to the airwaves at eleven fifteen. He spoke in a sober, melancholy tone.

"I am speaking to you from the Cabinet Room of 10 Downing Street," he began. Then he informed the country:

This morning the British Ambassador in Berlin handed the German Government a final Note stating that, unless we heard from them by 11 o'clock that they were prepared at once to withdraw their troops from Poland, a state of war would exist between us.

I have to tell you now that no such undertaking has been received and that, consequently this country is at war with Germany.[1]

Chamberlain then confessed:

You can imagine what a bitter blow it is to me that all my long struggle to win peace has failed. Yet I cannot believe that there is anything more or anything different that I could have done and that would have been more successful.

Up to the very last it would have been quite possible to have arranged a peaceful and honourable settlement between Germany and Poland, but Hitler would not have it. He had evidently made up his mind to attack Poland whatever happened, and although [h]e now says he put forward reasonable proposals which were rejected by the Poles, that is not a true statement. The proposals were never shown to the Poles, nor to us, and, although they were announced in a German broadcast on Thursday night, Hitler did not wait to hear comments on them, but ordered his troops to cross the Polish frontier. His action shows convincingly that there is no chance of expecting that this man will ever give up his practice of using force to gain his will. He can only be stopped by force. . . .

The situation in which no word given by Germany's ruler could be trusted and no people or country could feel [itself] safe has become intolerable. And now that we have resolved to finish it, I know that you will all play your part with calmness and courage. . . .

May God bless you all. And may He defend the right. It is the evil things that we shall be fighting against—brute force, bad faith, injustice, oppression and persecution— and against them I am certain that the right will prevail.[2]

Within half an hour after this announcement, as if to persuade the nation that their worst fears were now realized, the air-raid sirens sounded.

False Alarm?

The sirens were triggered by a French fighter plane, which had inadvertently flown into British airspace and set off the hyper-attentive alarms. The average person couldn't have known that. Chamberlain's announcement was like a shot from a starting pistol for a race between raw nerves and fear. Germany *would* invade. Everyone knew it. *But so soon?* they wondered. The sirens told them *yes.*

Families scrambled for the shelters. Some people rushed from churches in the middle of services. Others rushed *toward* churches for shelter or prayer or both. Half-dressed men and women dashed into the streets to see what was happening in the sky above. Some reached places of safety only to be dismayed that the gas masks they'd been given weren't accessible, having been buried in a box somewhere in a closet back home.

Few were prepared. Most were panicked.

At the BBC, the internal alarm system went off. Joseph Macleod, a newsreader, described it as "the loudest, most ear-tearing, most soul-lacerating things I had ever heard."[3] Horrible bangs and bumps left him believing the entire building was being bombed to smithereens. When he later emerged and found everything intact and peaceful, he had to assume the noises were merely slamming doors as employees had raced to the concert hall, which now served as the air-raid shelter.[4]

In other parts of London, rumors spread that the entire East End had been devastated, killing thousands. In fact, no one had been hurt.

The same couldn't be said for British citizens elsewhere. Two hundred miles west of Scotland, the German submarine *U-30* torpedoed the British liner *Athenia*. It sank, killing 112 passengers, including at least 28 Americans.[5]

And so, for the people of Great Britain, the Second World War of the twentieth century began.

✳ ✳ ✳

Reverend James Welch understood why the Religious Broadcasting department had to relocate from London to Bristol, but he wasn't happy about it. He believed Religious Broadcasting needed to be relevant to the BBC's listeners, and to be relevant meant experiencing what many of them would experience. He had a difficult time believing they could do that from Bristol, so far away from London.

Relevance was a key concept for Welch. He wanted "the people of the country to realise that the Church was more than just a pious institution but had something to say to the . . . life of the nation as a whole."[6]

These weren't simply words for Welch; these were the convictions of a well-educated, passionate clergyman. An astute and thoughtful man, Welch viewed every job he'd ever taken as a mission to further the cause of Christ. To look at a photo of him, one sees the narrow face and intelligent eyes of an English vicar, the kind one might have seen in a 1930s film as played by a Leslie Howard or, in a more contemporary visual translation, a Hugh Laurie.

Joining Welch at the BBC was forty-year-old assistant director Eric Fenn, also an ecumenicalist and a minister in the English Presbyterian Church (though he wasn't fully licensed until 1943).

Together, Welch and Fenn found themselves at the forefront of a new age in broadcasting in general and religious broadcasting in particular. The outbreak of war, they both believed, meant the gospel should be more important than ever to the people of Britain. Welch asked, "How can we be true to the word of the living God of all the nations, and at the same time meet the needs and terrible anxieties of a nation responding to the demands of a total war?"[7]

ERIC FENN

Eric Fenn (1899–1995) was born in London, the fourth son of Louis and Jessie Mary Fenn.[8] Louis was a leader in the National Temperance League and would later become a bishop of the Free Church of England. The family moved from London to Birkenhead, where Eric attended Wallasey grammar school. He adopted the evangelical faith of his parents and, with the outbreak of the First World War, listed himself as a conscientious objector. As a result, he was sent first to Wormwood Scrubs Prison and later to Knutsford and Dartmoor Prisons, where he did hard labor until the end of the war. After his release, he nearly died from the 1918 Spanish flu pandemic. Like so many in his generation, his Christian faith was shattered by all he'd experienced. He turned to science for answers, studying chemistry and physics at Imperial College in London. The rise of a new generation of theologians, who gave more room for intelligence over pure dogmatism, attracted Fenn and eventually led him to Westminster College, Cambridge. There he found his faith renewed as he stopped thinking about God as a "theory" but as someone "who *is.*" After this experience, he sought ordination.

Fenn became involved in the Student Christian Movement (SCM), where he eventually became a meticulous secretary for its meetings and a full-time employee at its headquarters in London.

His sharp mind, organizational skills, and modest demeanor brought him to the attention of the organization that would later become the World Council of Churches, where he was enlisted to help assemble international conferences. In that capacity he encountered many of England's brightest theological minds, including John Baillie and Alec Vidler, and lay members such as T. S. Eliot, John Middleton Murry, philosophers H. A. Hodges and Michael Polanyi, and sociologist Karl Mannheim.

James Welch would have crossed paths with Fenn during these years and was probably impressed with Fenn's knowledge and connections. Welch hired Fenn for the BBC in 1939.

To answer that question in what might have been considered a "Christian" nation would have been difficult enough. But Britain had changed in the years leading up to the war—and so had the BBC.

The Faith of the Nation

Welch, in his foreword to Dorothy Sayers's published version of *The Man Born to Be King*, a radio play about the life of Christ, suggested that listeners in Britain were divided into three groups: "Those who approved of religious broadcasts, those who were indifferent but not unfriendly, and those who were positively hostile. The first group asked little more than the traditional presentation of the Christian religion through services and talks, though they asked that these should be good."[9] He determined that "the other groups were unmoved" and generally "unreached" by this traditional presentation.[10] He concluded several things:

1. The "dimension we call 'God'" had disappeared from people's lives, allowing them to live without faith or needing any sense of God in their decision making. God was an irrelevance.

2. The "language of religion" had lost its meaning, especially when it used the Shakespearean language of the King James Version.

3. Most people were ignorant of the Christian faith. For example, "[Of] a group of men entering the Army only 23 per cent knew the meaning of Easter," and one young man thought Mark's gospel was written by Karl Marx.

4. In spite of all this, a "widespread dissatisfaction with materialism" still drove people to spiritual yearnings, with the "consensus of opinion" that Jesus still provided the "key to many of the riddles of life."[11]

"There is no need to elaborate this analysis," Welch wrote. "Anyone who moves outside Church circles knows it to be substantially true."[12]

It's astonishing to remember that Welch was describing Great Britain in the early days of the Second World War—not post-atomic-bomb baby boomers or the later alphabetized generations.

This secularized culture was the audience Welch hoped could be reached in the name of Jesus Christ. With the declaration of war, he felt an urgency to demonstrate that the church and religious broadcasting could meet the needs of the people.

What he may not have appreciated was just how far the war would take the BBC itself from its founding principles.

The Founding of the BBC

The BBC was founded in 1922 as a private company, started by a group of wireless manufacturers who needed to give people a reason to buy their products. In 1927 it was given a royal charter and incorporated. Income was generated by selling licenses to listeners—sometimes as many as a thousand per day. It quickly became a core feature of British life.

The visionary behind the BBC's success was a thirty-three-year-old Scottish engineer named John Reith. His zeal, religious convictions, and undaunted determination were so formidable that the phrase *Reithian values* became synonymous for quality and integrity.

Reith believed the power of broadcasting as a scientific invention shouldn't be used for entertainment alone. Such a thing would have been "a prostitution of its powers and an insult to the character and intelligence of the people."[13] To ensure the BBC would be used in the best possible way, he established three pillars set firmly on the foundation of Reith's Christian faith: education, information, and entertainment.

It might surprise modern readers that in prewar Britain, religious programming accounted for more broadcasting hours than other types of programming. Sundays were treated as the Sabbath, with all broadcasting dedicated to religious services, allowing only brief interruptions for the weather forecast or the news.

But the war would significantly change the BBC's views about religious programming, much to Reverend Welch's alarm. Proving that his department was relevant and that religion could meet this crisis head-on became imperative.

His first opportunity arrived—and went terribly wrong.

John Reith's Vision

A gold inscription hangs on the lobby wall at the BBC's headquarters—the first thing a person sees when entering the building. The inscription, translated from Latin, announces Reith's vision:

> This temple of the arts and muses is dedicated to Almighty God by the first Governors [of Broadcasting] in the year of our Lord 1931, John Reith being Director-General. And they pray that good seed sown may bring forth good harvest, and that all things foul or hostile to peace may be banished thence, and that the people inclining their ear to whatsoever things are lovely and honest, whatsoever things are of good report, may tread the path of virtue and wisdom.[14]

There is also a sculpture at the back of the lobby called *The Sower* by Eric Gill. Beneath it, also in Latin, are inscribed the words "God gives the increase."[15]

Reith's foundational belief is captured in that one image: the seeds of Christianity should be *broadly cast* to all who have ears to hear.

The Archbishop's Speech

The archbishop of Canterbury, Cosmo Lang, was seventy-four on September 3, 1939. He had been one of the appeasers, along with Chamberlain, who believed peace would prevail. When Poland was invaded, Lang begrudgingly returned to London from his retreat in the Highlands of Scotland. He was despondent, physically ill, and, according to one biographer, unsure of how he might cope with the coming conflict.[16]

At 8:00 p.m. on September 3, Lang took to the microphone at the BBC's studios in Bristol. These were the first words the nation would hear from the head of its church. Welch was anxious that they would be encouraging and meaningful.

Few remember what Lang actually said. No written speech exists. But the general consensus seems to agree with Fenn's description: the speech was "vapid and totally irrelevant." Fenn's secretary, listening as the talk was delivered, turned to him and asked, "What on earth does that man think he's for?"[17]

The *Times* and the *Church Times* only acknowledged that a speech had been made but didn't bother to quote the archbishop at all.[18]

Welch and Fenn were deeply disappointed.

Knowing that something needed to be done to rectify the situation, Welch insisted that Fenn take a broadcast slot to deliver the message they wished the archbishop had given. Fenn agreed, though he felt impertinent to attempt it, and delivered a speech that caught the tone Welch wanted. Fenn began by admitting that with the start of the war, the British people might believe that God had disappointed them—that faith was in vain. He also reflected on the reality of death and how it might come to them on a large scale in the days ahead. One way or another, everyone must "come to terms with death," he said. Finally he expressed his belief that Christians could span the most "awful division of war" by uniting together.[19]

Fenn spoke in terms the average listener could understand. He empathized with their feelings and offered hope. In many ways his broadcast was a hint at the direction to come for religious broadcasting.

But it would take a long time to get there.

4

DÉJÀ VU

THE SECOND WAR BEGAN FOR Jack Lewis with a frustrating task. The experience reminded him of procedures from the first war in which information "comes too late to prevent you doing an unnecessary job."[1]

The job was to spend a handful of exhausting days moving all the books from his college rooms to the cellar of the college so the government could use the rooms as offices. The government reversed its decision, so Jack spent another handful of exhausting days returning the books to their rightful place.

Meanwhile he was still determined to do more for the war effort than merely teach students or wait to be summoned by the military for a job he might not want. He became a Local Defence Volunteer with the Oxford City Home Guard Battalion. If the Germans attempted to invade by parachute, it would be Jack's job to fight or capture the invaders. His shift began at one thirty every Saturday morning.

Jack's initial experiences on duty were reasonably enjoyable. Rather than going to bed only to wake up a couple of hours later, he chose to have late meals with friends before his designated time. For the three-hour shift itself, he was partnered with other men of varying ages and experience. Some were students with whom he engaged like the tutor he was. On one occasion he corrected a fellow sentry regarding the "purposes" of "nature." He argued that nature couldn't have purposes unless it was a "rational substance," and if it were rational, then he'd be better off calling it "God, or the gods, or a god, or the devil."[2]

Jack's exposure to people outside his normal circle increased his awareness of the "fog of nonsense"[3] that had affected the thinking of so many.

His greater delight in protecting Oxford at that hour was to find beauty he would otherwise have missed—bright moons over glistening fields, the spires of the city reaching up to starlit skies, rain washing the streets clean, the lonely sound of a train trundling past. Those sentiments didn't last, however. Lugging a rifle around marred his pleasure, as did the subsequent colds he picked up from the wet nights. Later he complained to good friend Arthur Greeves[4] about having to hang around the "most depressing and malodorous parts of Oxford."[5]

Nevertheless, Jack performed his duty faithfully whenever called upon. He remained anxious, however, because there was every chance he would still be called to the war.

❋ ❋ ❋

In September 1939, Jack talked to George Gordon, president of Magdalen College, for a second time. Rather than lament the possibility of being enlisted into military service, Jack put forward the suggestion that he would be best suited to instruct cadets, having done so in one way or another over the previous fifteen years.

Gordon countered with the idea that Jack ought to work for the Ministry of Information. Jack was alarmed by the suggestion. He said he wasn't interested in the kind of "shilly-shallying" such a job would require. Gordon reassured Jack that he would protest if such a thing happened. Yet again, Jack was left hanging—and waiting.[6]

The New Normal

Few modern Americans could know what life was like for the average British family during World War II. No aspect of normal living was left untouched by government regulations. Routines were completely disrupted, and new ways of living had to be established.

"The main trouble of life at present," Lewis wrote to Warnie, "is the blacking out which is done (as you may imagine) with a most complicated Arthur Rackham* system of odd rags—quite effectively but at the cost of much labor. Luckily I do most of the rooms myself, so it doesn't take me nearly so long as if I were assisted."[7]

Eliminating lights meant the German pilots couldn't use them as guides for fixed positions on the ground. Not that Oxford had anything to worry about. Few, if any, German planes went that way. A rumor emerged that Hitler had instructed the German air force not to attack university cities such as Oxford and Cambridge so they would be left for Germans to use after the invasion.

---

* Arthur Rackham (1867–1939) was a popular British illustrator of classic and children's books, who was known for his use of intricate layering of detailed lines and color.

The Recipe for Victory

Jack and The Kilns's handyman, Fred Paxford, might not have heard the rumor, or if they had, didn't believe it. Both were World War I veterans and well experienced in digging trenches. They found a spot in the side of a hill near the pond and dug out a shelter for the air raids.

Just after Germany's invasion of Poland, the British government took control of virtually everything—rationing food, fuel, and even clothes. Families were given coupon books to use in the shops; each coupon had a specific amount allowed for a specific item. The lines around the shops often stretched for blocks. The allowances for all foodstuffs—whether dairy, meat, poultry, or fish—were meager. People in the country were encouraged to eat rabbits, pigeons, and crows. Recipe books appeared with innovations on corned beef, cake recipes without eggs, mutton as a replacement bacon, one hundred cheese recipes, tips for making vegetables taste like meat, better uses for cabbage, sheep's head prepared with caper sauce, vegetable marrow with liver stuffing, sardine pancakes, chestnut soup, salmon in custard, and a tasty dish called *liver mould*.

According to a Ministry of Information pamphlet, waste was tantamount to treason. A woman and her housekeeper were fined for "wasting bread"—they'd been caught feeding it to the birds in their back garden.[8]

The government also launched the Dig for Victory campaign, encouraging everyone to create vegetable gardens within their gardens, or to use "allotments" in vacant fields. Paxford was well ahead of the scheme, having grown vegetables in The Kilns's gardens before the war began.

FRED PAXFORD

Fred Paxford[9] was the gardener and handyman for The Kilns, whom Jack and Mrs. Moore hired shortly after the house was bought in 1930. A confirmed bachelor, he lived in a bungalow on the estate and worked endlessly—and frugally—to maintain the grounds, fix anything that needed it, grow food in the garden and orchard, tend to the flowers, and even help Mrs. Moore with her chickens. He was intuitive, practical, and indispensible to everyone in the house. Jack called him his "indispensible fac-totum."*[10]

An "ever cheerful eternal pessimist,"[11] Paxford spoke in a broad country accent that communicated a remarkable gloom, though the man himself seemed free of actual worry. It was a remarkable incongruity. Paxford somehow found that the worst possible situation always had an upside that sounded even worse. Once, when a maid worried that there might not be enough sugar in the house if Jack entertained guests, Paxford observed, "Well, you never know when the end of the world will come and we don't want to be left with sugar on our hands. What'll we do with it then, eh?"[12]

Mrs. Moore treated Paxford's advice as gospel. And because he was the same age as Jack, Paxford respected Mrs. Moore as the true boss around the house.

Warnie found it exasperating.

Jack, on the other hand, found Paxford endlessly helpful and amusing and even modeled a character after Paxford in *The Silver Chair*: Puddleglum.

Though the events of Jack's life could be told without mentioning Paxford, this reliable and earthy man was as ever-present to Jack's world as the bricks and mortar of The Kilns itself—and as easy to take for granted.

---

* A *factotum* is a servant of versatile abilities and responsibilities.

The Kilns had its own coop of chickens as a source for food, rescuing residents and guests from the notoriously awful dried eggs that most homes had to eat.

On rare occasions Jack was able to bring home leftover food from friends or coworkers at the college.

Mrs. Moore and Fred Paxford had to manage The Kilns with all the shrewdness and cunning of Ebenezer Scrooge. Kilns's evacuees would later testify to the frugal menu: potatoes; an apple and a glass of milk; occasional English biscuits (cookies); and whatever vegetables Paxford happened to grow in the garden. The making of porridge was a nightly tradition. The pot would be left to cool overnight and the boiled grains eaten the next morning.

Mrs. Moore was notorious for hoarding butter, keeping the larder filled with as much as she could get her hands on. This wasn't as mad as it might seem, considering the initial per-person rationing allowed only four ounces of butter—and four of margarine—a week (the amount was later dropped to two ounces). But according to one evacuee who came later in the war, the volume of butter in the house never seemed to diminish.[13] Mrs. Moore's reasons were practical: butter was an essential ingredient for many of her dishes, and one never knew when it might run out. She wasn't wrong to be concerned. British staples such as tea and sugar eventually found their way onto the rations list—along with jam, marmalade, syrup, mincemeat, lemon curd, and honey.[14]

The new austerity facing the nation, along with the imminent threat of invasion and potential loss of life, weighed heavily on Jack. The previous war was still fresh in his memories. Yet he worked hard to maintain a constructive perspective.

Siege Cake

4 oz. dripping or lard
4 oz. moist sugar
4 oz. golden syrup
1½ teacupsful buttermilk
lemon flavouring
1 level teaspoon bicarbonate of soda
12 oz. flour

To save sugar, 6 oz. of syrup and 2 oz. of sugar can be used. If buttermilk is not available, use ordinary milk, 1 level teaspoon of cream of tartar, and ½ teaspoon of bicarbonate of soda.

Grease a cake-tin measuring about 7 inches in diameter. Beat fat, sugar, and golden syrup until the consistency of whipped cream; gradually work in the buttermilk. Sift the flour with bicarbonate of soda and work it lightly into the mixture. Add the lemon flavouring. Bake in a moderate oven for about 1¼ hours.[13]

"The next few years will be ghastly," he admitted to Arthur Greeves, "but though my *nerves* are often staggered, my faith and reason are alright. I have no doubt that all this suffering will be for our ultimate good if we use it rightly . . . but I can't help wishing one could *hibernate* till it's all over!"[16]

He then quoted Warnie from a previous letter:

What makes it worse is the ghostly feeling that it has all happened before—that one fell asleep during the last

war and had a delightful dream and has now waked up
again.

I daresay for me, personally, it has come in the nick
of time: I was just beginning to get too well settled in my
profession, too successful, and probably self complacent.[17]

His words were remarkably prophetic considering how everything would change for him.

True and False Alarms

An air-raid warning was "a wail lasting two minutes, consisting
of either a fluctuating or 'warbling' signal of varying pitch or a
succession of blasts of about 5 seconds' duration, broken up by
silent periods of about 3 seconds."[18]

When it sounded early one morning in that first week of war,
The Kilns's household quickly made their way to the dugout. It
was "the most perfect late summer morning I have ever seen," Jack
wrote.[19] The evacuees were well behaved, though everyone was
hungry and thirsty when the all clear sounded a few hours later.

False alarms soon became commonplace for most of the
people in Britain. In Oxford there would be far more false
alarms than actual raids. By the war's end, the only "bombing"
to take place near The Kilns happened after a lost and panicked
German pilot, eager to lessen his plane's weight to fly higher,
dumped his payload over the area.[20]

For now, though, the Germans were busy in other parts of
Europe. The newly declared war began anticlimactically, with
what looked like a lot of fuss about nothing. The Phony War
had begun.

THE VERY REAL PHONY WAR

ON SEPTEMBER 17, 1939, ONLY sixteen days after Germany invaded Poland from the west, the Russians invaded Poland from the east. As had been the case with the German invasion, there was no declaration of war by the Soviets—they argued that the Nazi invasion had caused the Polish government to collapse, thus threatening the Soviet citizens in that region.

Germany intensified its military efforts to claim the country from the north, west, and south. The Polish army retreated to the Romanian corner of their country and hoped to hold on until the Allies could help. On October 6, the Polish Republic's hope faded when its army was defeated at the Battle of Kock. Poland was now effectively in the hands of the Nazis and the Soviets—and would be until the Nazis drove out the Soviets in the summer of 1941.

Mrs. Moore, alarmed by the fall of Poland to the Soviets, determined that the fate of the Allies was now sealed and even "talked of buying a revolver!"[1]

Mrs. Moore's anxiety proved to be premature. The Germans were too busy to think about invading England as they secured

Poland and fortified the Siegfried Line along the French border to rebuff any possible attack.

The British and French, for their part, held on to the Maginot Line on the French side of the border. The two sides faced each other without either taking any substantial action. It was repetition of the First World War. Apart from a couple of bombings on the Orkney Islands, north of the coast of Scotland, in October and again the following March,[2] there were few other skirmishes to speak of. An uneasy quiet settled on Western Europe.

Wireless Revolution

Historian Asa Briggs noted that unlike later wars when television and film would play critical roles in public perception, the Second World War was "a war not of images but of words." And not just words but *spoken* words—and sounds—as "a shortage of newsprint . . . magazines and books . . . gave added power to words on the air."[3]

By the first year of the war, most of the British people owned or had access to a radio. For them, the BBC was their only local source of wireless information or entertainment, particularly since theaters, cinemas, and other venues had been closed for safety reasons at the start of the war. Families often left the radio on all day, playing in the background, as they went about their business.

The initial urgency of the war dissipated quickly when Germany didn't attack Britain. The ten news bulletins scheduled each day were soon superfluous as the Phony War left newsreaders with little to report.

Music was a mainstay of programming, from phonograph records or, when possible, live orchestras. The BBC pipe organ, played from the basement concert hall by Sandy Macpherson, filled in many of the gaps between programs. Government ministers took to the microphone to lecture and encourage listeners. Public announcements were given a solid hour each day.

The public, the press, even government ministers, were soon fed up with the banal content. The BBC began to receive blistering complaints. The *Sunday Times* called its programming "an endless stream of trivialities and sillinesses, apparently labouring under the delusion that in any time of crisis the British public becomes just one colossal moron."[4] It was even suggested that the BBC had become an effective weapon—for the Germans.

Two problems now faced the BBC and, specifically, James Welch. First, the content they were creating, and second, the presentation of that content.

Welch's instincts already told him things needed to change long before the complaints came, but he was powerless to do very much. Having been exiled to Bristol, his accessibility to speakers was limited. Only four religious speakers took to the microphone on a regular basis: James Welch; Eric Fenn; the dean of Bristol Cathedral, Harry Blackburne; and Rev. Sydney Swann of St. Mary Redcliffe Church.

Another limitation came in the form of censorship. Though the BBC was constitutionally independent, the government exerted detailed control over its broadcasts to ensure the Germans couldn't use the broadcast information to their advantage. Scripts were carefully checked and rechecked by BBC employees and government censors. Speakers were required to follow scripts to the letter. Any variance or impromptu comments meant the engineer was authorized to pull the plug.

The government also took a dim view of speakers espousing pacifist beliefs. The government's argument was simple: In a time of war, when building the nation's morale is critical, it's counterproductive to have pacifists whispering in the ears of listeners about not fighting when they were needed to fight. The government reasoned that since the idealistic appeasers had failed to thwart the conflict, how would the pacifists help the nation win it? Pacifist speakers, popular before the war, suddenly disappeared from the airwaves.

The BBC's board of directors and its subordinate Central Religious Advisory Committee served as the bridge between the corporation and the government. The two entities had their share of arguments over content and on-air personalities. More than once, Welch and Fenn came close to resigning.

As if those issues weren't difficult enough, Welch had to deal with a setback that would change religious broadcasting permanently.

The Other Mrs. Moore

In November 1939, death came to The Kilns.

Mrs. Alice Hamilton Moore,[5] no relation to Mrs. Janie Moore or even of Jack on the Hamilton side of his family, was the widow of a doctor in Bushmills, Ireland, and a friend of the family. She'd come upon difficult times and bad health, so Jack and Minto invited her to live in a small bungalow on The Kilns property.

Alice Moore soon plummeted into what Jack called a "brain storm," possibly a form of dementia. She was nursed by Minto and a close friend and neighbor to The Kilns. Her health improved marginally. On Thursday, November 2, she complained of feeling uncomfortable—"only middling"[6]—but mostly at ease. Then she passed away.

The complexities of her death and funeral arrangements consumed everyone in the house until November 6, when she was buried at Headington Quarry's Holy Trinity Church. Jack paid for everything out of his own pocket.

In a letter to Warnie, who had now shipped off to France, Jack noted how his view of funerals had changed since his conversion to Christianity:

> One has lost, in a great measure, one's old morbid feeling about funerals: and what a satisfaction it is to find that the new outlook has, in even one direction, worked down as far as the level of the instinctive feelings. Would that it were so in *all* directions. What I still find most untouched is the speech habits—I meant that in the full tide of conversation one still finds oneself saying automatically things that are uncharitable, profane, and even untrue.[7]

The reality of Alice Moore's death—and the introspection it caused within Jack—had a timely connection to a book he'd just agreed to write.

The Problem of Pain

Centenary Press, an imprint of London's Geoffrey Bles, Ltd. (which would later publish most of Jack's books in England), was a small publishing house specializing in religious topics. Ashley Sampson, its founder, had read an early book by Jack called *The Pilgrim's Regress*. He liked it enough to approach Jack about writing a book as part of a collection called the Christian Challenge series. The series dealt with subjects as diverse as evil, immortality, social action, psychology, moral conduct, and

Christianity's relationship to other religions. Sampson wanted Jack to tackle the subject of pain. The purpose of the book was to "solve the intellectual problem raised by suffering."[8]

Jack approached the project with great humility, being aware of his own theological limitations, yet desiring to tackle the subject for his own sake as well as his readers'. He worried that this generation might reject God in the aftermath of the war, just as his generation had after the First World War. The people of Britain needed help with the subject of pain *now*.

The challenge was also enticing. How could he work through the problem of suffering in a way that would be meaningful to an average reader? His personal integrity as an academic demanded that he construct a logical and thorough argument, while his convictions as a Christian demanded that he avoid easy or sentimental answers. More than anything, the book had to be meaningful to his readers.

Considering what he endeavored to do, it's remarkable to think that less than a decade before this, Jack hadn't believed in Christianity at all.

Reluctant Convert

Jack's spiritual journey, which he later chronicled in *Surprised by Joy*, was an intellectually and emotionally complex one, integrating his mind, heart, and imagination in unique ways.

Raised in a house filled with books, Jack had an imagination that was stimulated from an early age. His mother taught him the Christian faith, but her death when he was nine years old caused him to doubt a God that could, but would not, heal her. His father, grief-stricken, volatile, and aloof, sent Jack and his brother off to a boarding school in England, where Jack's experience resembled a nightmare from a Dickens novel. His circumstances improved when he moved on to an English preparatory school, but his faith did not. He was drawn closer to atheism and developed an interest in the occult, especially the prevalent forms of preternatural spiritualism that included contact with the dead.

At fifteen, Jack won a place at Malvern College and entered into a particularly unhappy experience—in part because he didn't fit in with the college's emphasis on sports.[9] There he concluded that God didn't exist at all, yet he was angry at God for *not* existing and, worse, for creating a world as bad as this one.[10]

Jack left Malvern in 1914 and was sent to live with a personal tutor—William Kirkpatrick, or the "Great Knock,"[11] whose atheism and intense logical discipline seemed the perfect place for Jack at this time of his life. Kirkpatrick challenged the logic of everything Jack said. No word was too incidental, no thought too slight to be fiercely debated. Now sixteen, Jack thrived on this kind of dynamic, as he would throughout the rest of his life when arguing with friends and adversaries.

Jack's atheism could have been set then and there, since the influence of Kirkpatrick brought out the best in him intellectually. But on a trip to a bookstore in a nearby town, Jack happened to pick up a fantasy novel called *Phantastes* by a writer named George MacDonald.[12] MacDonald was a nineteenth-century Scottish minister who made his living as a teacher, lecturer, and writer. His books included collections of sermons, essays, fiction, and of more importance to Jack, fantasies and fairy tales. Jack delighted in the sheer imaginative power of what he read, without knowing there was a Christian undercurrent to all of it. MacDonald would become one of the greatest literary influences in Jack's life.

The First World War nearly clinched Jack's conviction that God, if He existed, wasn't "good" in any way at all. But while recuperating from trench fever in a French hospital, Jack read a collection of essays by G. K. Chesterton.[13] Though he disagreed with Chesterton's theology, he was drawn in by the "goodness" of the writing. Both Chesterton and MacDonald baptized Jack's imagination.

Back in Oxford after the war, Jack rejected God but accepted absolute idealism, a view that acknowledged the possibility of a meaningful universe but without an "Absolute"—a God or whatever it might be—coming into the world to "make a nuisance of Itself [with demands or laws]." And, "there was nothing to fear; better still, nothing to obey."[14]

A friendship with Owen Barfield in 1919 challenged Jack's view of God. Barfield, training to be a lawyer, argued with Jack about the supernatural, in general, and, more specifically, the idea of a personal God. Barfield also attacked a popular view at the time, which Jack had adopted, that all things modern were unequivocally legitimate, while anything from the past was readily discredited. Jack eventually conceded to Barfield's point of view that the past was not *always* wrong—there might be some merit in old ideas and philosophies. This opened the door for the possibility that the historical Christian message could be valid.

Jack read a well-known Christian author and concluded that "Christianity was very sensible apart from its Christianity."[15] He read the Gospels and found them compelling as truth only because he considered the authors too artless and unimaginative to have made the stories up as myth. Yet the idea of a personal God still eluded him.

He began to teach philosophy, which required him to be more specific about what the "Absolute" in his absolute idealism actually was. One day, on a bus, Jack had a nagging feeling that, in his thinking, he was holding a door closed—a door he could open if he wanted to. Without knowing what the feeling meant, he decided to open the door. From then on, his arguments against a personal God fell apart.

"You must picture me alone in that room in Magdalen," he wrote in *Surprised by Joy*:

> . . . night after night, feeling, whenever my mind lifted even for a second from my work, the steady, unrelenting approach of Him whom I so earnestly desired not to meet. That which I greatly fear had at last come upon me. In the Trinity Term* of 1929 I gave in, and admitted that God was God, and knelt and prayed: perhaps, that night, the most dejected and reluctant convert in all England.[16]

The death of his father on September 24, 1929, affected Jack deeply. Guilt over their rocky relationship and how he had treated his father over the years weighed heavily on him. He was ashamed. He believed he had deep character deficiencies that ought to be corrected. He also sensed that his father was actually *helping* him from beyond the grave to work on his flaws. To

---

* In 1929, the third term, known at Oxford as the Trinity Term, began the week of April 15.

admit that possibility meant he had to admit there was more to reality than an easy notion of God as a benevolent, but distant, being.

At roughly the same time, Warnie was on a similar spiritual journey while serving in the British army in Asia. The two brothers didn't know of their parallel explorations. It wasn't until Warnie's arrival back in England in the spring of 1930 that they had time to discuss and debate their changing views about God. They began to read the Bible regularly and attend their local Church of England parish on Sundays.

The turning point for Jack came on September 19, 1931, when he had dinner with friends and fellow Oxford teachers J. R. R. Tolkien[17] and Hugo Dyson.[18] Over the meal they talked about myths, a subject Jack and "Tollers" (Tolkien's nickname) enjoyed deeply. Afterward they took a stroll along Addison's Walk near the college. Tolkien impressed upon Jack the view that myths weren't entirely untrue, as Jack believed, but came from God and expressed part of God's truth, though it might be distorted. Tolkien also suggested that by writing and creating myths, man* was participating in God's work of creation.

As Tolkien spoke, a mysterious rush of wind through the trees seemed to speak to Jack, like a whisper from God Himself.

Tolkien pressed on with his argument: the Christian story was a myth, but a true one, created by a true God who became man and died on the cross to transform those who believed in Him.

Hugo Dyson picked up the gauntlet, adding that Christianity frees a man from himself—his sins—and works to bring about a new person.

---

* Terms such as *man* and *mankind* were used in the 1940s and assumed to include both men and women.

The arguments of his two friends struck Jack deeply. Suddenly his intellectual mind, his imagination, and his guilt-ridden heart were unified in one search for truth.

A few days later Jack admitted to Arthur Greeves that he had moved from his general theistic position toward belief in Jesus Christ. Then, in a bizarre fashion, he made a further decision while riding in the sidecar of his brother's motorcycle on the way to the Whipsnade Zoo. He later wrote, "When we set out I did not believe that Jesus Christ is the Son of God, and when we reached the zoo I did."[19]

He described the experience as being like a man who had been asleep for a very long time and, while "lying motionless in bed," realized he was now awake.[20]

Though Jack still had questions and doubts about Christianity, he embarked on a new relationship with Christ. He studied and explored the faith with the same tenacity and diligence as he had while trying to refute it. He attended his local parish church and would eventually use the essential theological beliefs of the Church of England as the springboard to develop his own ideas, creating a style and approach that would appeal to Christians of all stripes. This appeal would play an important role in the book *The Problem of Pain* and everything he created afterward.

Open on Sundays

The BBC Home Service—which combined the corporation's national and regional broadcasting at the start of the war— languished under the weight of news and information. As the Phony War continued, the BBC took time to evaluate its overall programming with a specific desire to meet the needs of the troops who were currently sitting idle in France. The BBC's British Forces Broadcasting Service (BFBS) was developed and launched early in 1940. Light entertainment returned to the airwaves with stars and shows that had been popular before the war. The producers held to the view that what was good for the soldiers abroad was good for everyone at home—including listeners of religious programming.

Leading up to Christmas 1939, the board of governors altered the BBC's Sunday policy. Where Sundays had been respected as the Sabbath and broadcasting limited to religious services and weather bulletins, now the airwaves would be opened up to regular programming: reruns of variety shows, dance music, and sports. Arguably, expanding the Sunday broadcast schedule was a practical decision. On that day the BBC usually lost up to half its audience to the radio stations from other countries, including Ireland, France, and Luxembourg.

Though James Welch was head of the Religious Broadcasting department, he wasn't consulted on the change and viewed it with alarm. He privately quipped, "I cannot see . . . why we should assume that because a few listeners have put on uniform and crossed the [English] Channel they should be considered different persons religiously."[21] Battle makes men more religious, he argued, not less so. He also complained that the decision was "based on expediency not principle."[22]

The underlying concern for Welch was that religious programming would now be judged by a different standard—it would no longer be measured by spiritual depth or insight, but by how many laughs it generated, or goose bumps, or tears.

Welch also knew his department would now have to com-

pete for time slots. Inevitably, he suspected, religious programming would be decreased in favor of pure entertainment. He
was right. Very quickly the midnight news on the Home Service
took over the devotional end-of-day epilogue. And the comedy
Happidrome broadcast on the British Forces Broadcasting Service competed directly with the religious program on the Home
Service.[23]

Welch didn't have an ally in his boss, Sir Frederick Ogilvie.
As the director general of the BBC since 1938, Ogilvie was the
antithesis of his predecessor Sir John Reith. A warm, educated,
and soft-spoken man, Ogilvie was more comfortable in an academic setting than fighting the battles he encountered at the
wartime BBC. He and Welch had a respectful relationship, but
Ogilvie sided with those who believed programming had to be
competitive and responsive to listeners. Unlike Reith, who offered what he believed the audience *needed*, Ogilvie conceded
to give audiences what they *wanted*. Unfortunately, they didn't
seem to want religious programming.[24]

The tide had turned for Welch and the BBC's Religious
Broadcasting department. He would now have to think about
religious broadcasting in an entirely different way. He had to
beat entertainment at its own game. But how?

To find out, Ogilvie sent Welch to talk to the soldiers in
France.

The Home Front

Jack established a semblance of prewar routine during the Phony
War. He taught, he wrote, he read, he volunteered—and he met
with his friends the Inklings.[25]

The Inklings

In his 1966 memoir of Jack, Warnie Lewis described the Inklings as "a famous and heroic gathering, one that has already passed into literary legend."[26] It was "neither a club nor a literary society, though it partook of the nature of both. There were no rules, officers, agendas, or formal elections—unless one counts it as a rule that we met in Jack's rooms at Magdalen every Thursday evening after dinner."[27] They also met on Tuesdays at various pubs around Oxford, the most popular being the Eagle and Child (nicknamed the "Bird and Baby") near the center of the city. According to Warnie, there was no fixed hour for the start of the gathering in Jack's rooms, "though there was a tacit agreement that ten-thirty was as late as one could decently arrive."[28] They met at the pub an hour before lunch.

Members came and went as schedules permitted. "We all knew the type of man we wanted or did not want,"[29] Warnie wrote. That type of man generally included a sharp and creative intellect, an academic pedigree, and, for some, a Christian worldview. Members included Jack, J. R. R. Tolkien, Hugo Dyson, Owen Barfield,[30] R. A. "Humphrey" Havard,[31] Nevill Coghill,[32] Charles Wrenn,[33] and Charles Williams.[34] Others came and went as they could; more joined after the war years.

In Jack's rooms, a cold meal was often provided, along with tea. Tobacco pipes would then be lit, and the gathering would hear readings from the members. During the war, Tolkien read from his work on The Lord of the Rings, Charles Williams often read from one of his plays or novels in progress, while, in that first year of war, Jack took the opportunity to read from *The Problem of Pain*.

The readings led to unbridled criticism and discussion. "Praise for good work was unstinted," Warnie recalled, "but censure for bad work—or even not-so-good work—was often brutally frank. To read to the Inklings was a formidable ordeal."[35]

Jack was the unofficial sun around which the Inklings orbited. His talk was "an outpouring of wit, nonsense, whimsy, dialectical swordplay, and pungent judgement."[36]

The conversation of the Inklings was exactly what one might expect from a group of friends at this time: They talked about the war, the university, friends and family being called to service, theology, health, stories, and anecdotes. Humor was a large part of every conversation.

Jack recounted to Warnie a story he'd heard about a dinner that "old Phelps," the provost of Oriel College, had with a fellow of Jesus College named Jenner. Now Jenner was a "fanatical tee-totaller," so when the provost asked Jenner to have some wine with him, Jenner replied, "Sir, I would rather commit adultery than drink a glass of *that*." To which Phelps replied in a stern voice, "So would we all, Jenner; but not at the table, if you please."[37]

In one contentious meeting, Charles Wrenn expressed the wish that Williams ought to be burned at the stake—or allowed that it could seem right to burn people for blasphemous views. Jack wrote, "Tolkien and I agreed afterwards that we *just* knew what he meant" in that, just "as some people at school are eminently kickable" by virtue of their personalities, "so Williams is eminently combustible."[38]

Jack's relationships and personal experiences made him keenly aware of the very human trends that emerged in a time of crisis. He knew how war often muddied clear thinking—and he was quick to challenge anyone who slipped into sentimentality or presumption.

Early in the conflict, for example, he reprimanded the vicar of his church, who had stated in a public prayer that God was on the side of their "righteous cause." He cautioned the minister "against the audacity of informing God that our cause was righteous—a point on which He may have His own view."[39]

Jack was also wary of how fascism or communism might use the war to penetrate Christianity, filling a vacuum of much-needed "good" with a dangerous imitation. "Mark my words," he wrote to a friend. "You will presently see both a Leftist and a Rightist pseudo-theology developing."[40]

The downside to Jack's rigorous intellect and his encounters with those around him was a sense of alienation. He wrote to Warnie, "I am afraid the truth is in this, as in nearly everything else I think about at present, that the world, as it is now becoming and has partly become, is simply *too much for* people of the old square-rigged type like you and me. I don't understand its economics, or its politics, or [anything] about it."[41]

Not only did the world's economics and politics confound Jack, but he was also alarmed by the kind of faith he began to see in the young Christians around Oxford. He disliked their "horrible ferocity and grimness of modern thought."[42] While imagining that *he* was the "upholder of the old, stern doctrines against modern quasi-Christian slush," he discovered that "*my* 'sternness' was *their* 'slush.'"

He wrote to Warnie that he was distressed to find everyone reading "a dreadful man called Karl Barth"[43] and talking like "Old Testament prophets," placing everyone "under judgment" without any regard for human reason or conscience. "They maintain, as stoutly as Calvin, that there's no reason why God's dealings should appear just (let alone merciful) to us: and they maintain the doctrine that *all* our righteousness is filthy rags with a fierceness and sincerity which is like a blow in the face."[44]

Challenging Assumptions

C. S. Lewis loved to challenge assumptions. Accounts from those who knew him—and quips that are pervasive throughout his letters—point to a man who sharpened his own thinking by sharpening the thinking of those around him. At this time he had an exchange of letters with his good friend Owen Barfield about the degree to which a man and a Christian "ought to be vividly and continuously aware"[45] of the sufferings going on overseas during the war. It's easy to believe that most people would accept the inherent truth of this sentiment. Not Jack Lewis. He countered that the "rapidity of communications etc. imposed a burden on sympathy for which sympathy was never made: that the natural thing was to be distressed about what was happening to the poor Jones's in *your own village*,"[46] whereas sympathy for the international difficulties, brought to the doorstep through journalism, "really *could not* be met in the same way."[47] Even if it could, Jack saw little point in being miserable on behalf of those overseas, since it would do them little good.

Years later, Clifford Morris—a man who often chauffeured Jack—recalled an occasion while driving through Oxford when someone suddenly ran in front of the car, forcing Morris to hit the brakes hard. Morris muttered something about "blessed pedestrians." With a twinkle in his eye, Jack immediately challenged him about his use of the word *blessed* and said, "I suspect that what you *really* meant was *damned pedestrians*—just the opposite to what you said! You certainly didn't hope that they were exceedingly happy now, and that presently they will enjoy the bliss of the celestial realms!"[48]

Through this particular brand of Christianity, Jack was persuaded that a "real red-hot Christian revival, with iron dogma, stern discipline, and ruthless asceticism" was far more possible than he had imagined. And "if it comes, people like us will not find it nearly so agreeable as we had expected."[49]

He wryly suggested to Warnie that they should start a "Stagnation Party" in which, during its term of office, "*no* event of the least importance" would take place.[50] With similar wryness, Jack wistfully lamented the loss of happier days when politics were no more complicated than tariff reform, a war was with the Zulus, and religion meant piety.

Behind all his observations, Jack knew the war was changing everything. The world he had known was slipping away from him. He feared his brother was too, as Warnie shipped off to France with the Fourth Company Seventh Divisional Train, British Expeditionary Force on November 4, 1939. Jack described it as a "sad business for us both, since he was retired and we had both hoped these partings were over."[51]

Even Mrs. Moore, who was usually preoccupied with the little crises she created at The Kilns, found the war digging into her subconscious. She lay awake one night during a storm, thinking vividly of those at sea and the nightmare of being torpedoed on such a night. The next morning brought the news that a neutral Dutch liner carrying four hundred men, women, and children was sunk by the Germans.[52]

If there was any relief for Jack and Mrs. Moore, it was the arrival of Jack's forty-first birthday on November 29. He was no longer eligible to be drafted into the military.

He wasn't called to service, but he was called to serve. The preparation for the work ahead came slowly.

The Practice of Pain

During the writing of *The Problem of Pain*, Jack slipped in the bathtub and hurt himself badly enough to wonder if he'd broken a rib. The pain reminded him of how he had felt in the casualty ward after being wounded in the First World War.[53]

Later he mused, "If you are writing a book about pain and then get some actual pain as I did from my rib, it does *not* either, as the cynic would expect, blow the doctrine to bits, nor, as a Christian would hope, turn into practice, but remains quite unconnected and irrelevant, just as any other bit of actual life does when you are reading or writing."[54]

In the book itself he wrote,

All arguments in justification of suffering provoke bitter resentment against the author. You would like to know how I behave when I am experiencing pain, not writing books about it. You need not guess, for I will tell you; I am a great coward. But what is that to the purpose? When I think of pain—of anxiety that gnaws like fire and loneliness that spreads out like a desert, and the heartbreaking routine of monotonous misery, or again of dull aches that blacken our whole landscape or sudden nauseating pains that knock a man's heart out at one blow, of pains that seem already intolerable and then are suddenly increased, of infuriating scorpion-stinging pains that startle into maniacal movement a man who seemed half dead with his previous tortures . . . [i]f I knew any way of escape I would crawl through sewers to find it. But what is the good of telling you about my feelings? You know them already: they are the same as yours. I am not arguing that pain is not painful. Pain hurts. That is what the word means. I am only trying to show that the old Christian doctrine of being made "perfect through suffering" is not incredible. To prove it palatable is beyond my design.[55]

The voice and technique Jack would use in his writings was evident as he integrated himself, the realities of life, and spiritual truth. A few years later he stated, "I have come to the conviction that if you cannot translate your thoughts into uneducated language, then your thoughts were confused. Power to translate is the test of having really understood one's own meaning."[56]

Mastering the vernacular would become a personal mission for Jack, though it wouldn't always come easily to him, as he was soon to discover.

6

CROSSING THE LINE

By THE END OF 1939, the average German had already suffered twenty years of financial hardship thanks to the outcome of the First World War. With this second war, seventy million of them—the civilians—were allowed meat and butter only twice a week and often subsisted on a diet of stuffed cabbage or boiled potatoes. Fuel rationing gave them hot water for just the weekends. Though they would never say so aloud, the Germans were tired of Hitler's war. According to a visiting American journalist, they considered Germany in the war the way a man considers a bad toothache: "the sooner it [was] out the better."[1]

Hitler had no intention of stopping his aggressive push through Europe, in spite of his military forces being stalled by one of the harshest winters they'd seen in forty-six years. He was determined to take Holland and Belgium. And then he planned to use their airfields to attack that pesky Great Britain—a stubborn nation that had unreasonably rejected his peace offer back in October. Give them a solid beating, he believed, and they would be more willing to negotiate. He would send in his mighty Luftwaffe to administer a healthy dose of discipline.[2]

The Superior German Planes

The *Luftwaffe* (German for "air force") was the powerful and highly effective air arm of the Third Reich. Assembled in defiance of the Treaty of Versailles after Hitler became German chancellor in 1933, the Luftwaffe was developed by Hermann Goering, Hitler's trusted deputy, and Erhard Milch, the director of the commercial airline Lufthansa. The two men organized their air branch into groups of fighter planes, bombers, night fighters, fast bombers, dive-bombers, and transports. Planes were built using the latest technology and designs for speed and stealth. By 1935, the Luftwaffe comprised more than eighteen hundred aircraft of all types, with over twenty thousand officers and enlisted men.[3]

In August 1936, the Luftwaffe made its debut supporting General Francisco Franco in the Spanish Civil War. Pilots gained much-needed practical experience in flying and tactical techniques. From that war, the traditional wing-to-wing formations—large groups of planes flying in close proximity—were abandoned for smaller groupings, and greater freedom was given to pilots to navigate independently.[4]

Among the many new planes Germany produced, two seemed especially invincible. The single-seat Messerschmitts (Me-109) had an eleven-hundred-horsepower, liquid-cooled engine and achieved speeds of more than 350 miles per hour while using two twenty-millimeter cannons and two 7.9-millimeter machine guns to quickly destroy the enemy. The Stukas, single-engine dive-bombers, also known as Junkers (Ju-87), had engines as powerful as the Messerschmitts but made only 232 miles per hour thanks to the eleven hundred pounds of bombs they carried.[5]

Two older bombers did their fair share of damage to Germany's enemies: the Dornier-17 (Do-17)—nicknamed the "Flying Pencil" because of its slender fuselage—achieved speeds of 265 miles per hour, with a bomb capacity of twenty-two hundred pounds; and the Heinkel He-111 with its fifty-five hundred pounds of bomb power.[6]

The German war strategy relied heavily on the blitzkrieg, which used the Luftwaffe's formidable air power as part of a surprise attack to clear the way for ground troops and tanks. The invasion of Poland showed the strengths of Hitler's methods. Sixteen hundred aircraft decimated the Polish strongholds and troops. Very few Polish pilots could get their planes off the ground thanks to the incessant bombing from the Stukas. Those pilots who managed to get airborne were quickly brought down again by the Messerschmitts.[7]

Goering had little doubt that his Luftwaffe could easily dominate the skies over Great Britain and bring the country to its knees.[8]

In Britain, Neville Chamberlain and his government hoped the Germans would exhaust themselves and give up on war. Others in his cabinet and war offices argued for a pact with Hitler, reasoning that the Nazis were the only buffer between them and another threat: Bolshevism.

The war thus far had cost Britain twenty-four million dollars a day and was an anticlimactic inconvenience. More people died each day from blackout-related accidents than armed conflict.[9] According to a survey by the Ministry of Information, approximately four million Britons were willing to settle for "peace at any price."[10]

Had they looked more closely at the war raging in Finland, they might have realized that peace at any price meant no peace at all.

✳ ✳ ✳

In November 1939, Russia invaded Finland. The Finnish fought back valiantly, but after 105 days of battle, they were exhausted and outnumbered by the superior forces from the east. Finland surrendered on March 12, 1940. The next day Finnish white-and-blue flags were moved to half-mast. Shortly afterward, more than five hundred thousand Finns had to vacate their homes in the twenty-five thousand square miles of land demanded for possession by the Russians.[11]

The fall of Finland led to a period of self-loathing among its allies. The Swedish reluctantly acknowledged that they had sacrificed Finland to preserve their own peace. The British, who had promised weapons to Finland's military, had delivered only a fraction of the amount they'd promised. Chamberlain's government had also stalled on allowing British volunteers to fight in Finland. In truth, Chamberlain had hedged his bets in a vain hope to win Russia away from its alliance with Germany.

It wasn't the only moment of weakness and folly by the British government during that long winter. Shortly after the war began, Winston Churchill—the first lord of the admiralty and a constant thorn in the flesh to Chamberlain—recognized that the so-called neutral nations of Finland, Sweden, and Norway could survive only if they stood up to Germany and Russia. "Each one hopes that if he feeds the crocodile enough, the crocodile will eat him last," he stated in a radio address. "All of them hope that the storm will pass before their turn comes to be devoured."[12]

Churchill began an internal campaign to persuade Chamberlain's war cabinet to place mines in Norway's territorial waters. Churchill believed this tactic would prevent the flow of Swedish iron ore from reaching Germany via the Norwegian port of Narvik.

Few sided with Churchill, arguing that the world would be outraged by such a violation of Norway's neutrality. Churchill was undaunted and raised the idea again in January 1940. Chamberlain, ever-weakening, allowed plans to be developed for not one but two operations involving Norway. The first was called Operation Wilfred, in which the British would mine Norway's waters—with or without Norway's permission. The second operation—named Plan R.4—involved British forces actually *invading* key cities in Norway and then destroying the ore fields in Sweden, in case the Germans retaliated over the mining operations.

Chamberlain worried that the allies would condemn bullying a small neutral nation. He argued that Britain had entered the war on moral grounds, and its credibility would be undermined by Churchill's plans. Churchill countered that Germany and Russia regularly disregarded the rules of war as it suited them, and Britain must consider doing the same for the sake of freedom. The war cabinet was fractured on the issue. The French made it clear they wanted no part of it.

Finland's surrender to the Germans in March intensified the debate. Chamberlain conceded to Churchill. Operation Wilfred was to launch in early April.

The British had no idea how ineffective their efforts would prove to be. The Germans had other plans.

✳ ✳ ✳

On April 6, 1940, a Swedish liner arrived in the harbor at Bergen, Norway. Passengers on board noted twenty German ore freighters anchored nearby. From all appearances, the freighters were deserted, sitting in the harbor like ghost ships. The passengers couldn't know that hundreds of German soldiers were hiding in the holds—and waiting.

On April 8, truck drivers from Denmark reported seeing a thirty-five-mile-long column of German troops marching toward the Danish frontier.

Four German coal ships sat in the waters near Copenhagen. Two thousand German troops hid inside.[13]

A vast array of German warships moved into the channel between Sweden and Denmark. By 11:30 p.m. they entered Oslo Fjord.[14]

Under the pretense of protecting Denmark from a French and British "invasion," the Germans crossed the Danish frontier on April 9, thus breaking Hitler's promise to respect Denmark's neutrality. The Danes could do very little. The seventy-year-old King Christian X couldn't bear the slaughter of his people and put a halt to any resistance. A "bloodless occupation"[15] took place.

In Norway the Germans quickly secured the five major cities and ports in the west and south. But King Haakon VII, Christian X's brother, refused to yield, choosing instead to move his government north to the city of Hamar to direct fighting from there.[16] In a bizarre lapse of communication, the Norwegian leadership failed to use the radio to alert its citizens of the invasion. Instead, they sent out messages by couriers. The average Norwegian saw frantic activity but had no idea the Germans were at the door.

As the facts emerged, few in Norway could hope to withstand the onslaught of the German military machine. Their hope was that the British and French would come to their aid.

✳ ✳ ✳

The BBC's director of religion was not idle during this time. James Welch went to France to talk to Allied soldiers firsthand about the BBC's programming. He was pleased and challenged by what he learned there.

In his subsequent report to the BBC's director general, Welch described the men he met as young, intelligent, and "surprisingly literate" (because of the long daily letters they wrote home), "not cranky, unbiased, not wedded to the familiar and reminiscent, ready and eager for experiments in broadcasting."[17]

Welch noted that in the midst of the "stupidity and frightfulness of war" these men were passionate about home and anything to do with home. He felt this made the BBC even more important to the soldiers. He was pleased to discover a lot of goodwill toward the BBC in general and its programming specifically. "They listen as few people at home listen—they have little else to do," he wrote.[18] The radio stayed on all the time, often as background noise, while the soldiers went about other business. More intentional listening happened in their private quarters.

In Welch's opinion, the men wanted to be entertained and yearned for anything that would break up the monotony of the incessant waiting for war, along with the dull "sameness" of their lives as soldiers. "Any contrast to army life is welcomed," he wrote.[19]

As for the Sunday Forces Programme, the opinions ranged from "For heaven's sake entertain us on Sunday, don't bore us" to "The more we live in France the more British we feel, and now we appreciate the British Sunday and desperately want it to be different from other days."[20] Yet again came the appeal to keep the programming from being dull.

Welch concluded that two audiences existed where religious broadcasting was concerned: "Those who wonder what the Church can say in wartime and are keen to criticize, and those who wish to be reminded of church services at home."[21]

Welch made several suggestions in his report about changes to the BBC's religious broadcasts for the forces. Behind his frontline experience, he knew he had to explore creative alternatives to traditional religious programs if he expected to keep his audience. Before he could do anything of substance, however, the situation in Europe changed dramatically.

✳ ✳ ✳

On April 15, 1940, more than twenty thousand British troops sailed in warships to Norway. While Churchill had given them the mandate to "purge and cleanse the soil . . . from the filthy pollution of Nazi tyranny,"[22] conflicting orders came from the war office about how to do that. General Mackesy, the commander, was besieged with communications giving him pointless detail—how to negotiate the purchase of ponies, for example—while leaving out more important information about his own military might.[23]

The British forces were ill-equipped and unprepared. Within four days of their arrival, they were easily repelled by the German war machine, which inflicted heavy casualties.

Jack watched the unfolding events and wondered with a "particular horror" what would happen with a summer campaign in Norway—with "*no* darkness: 24 hours' war out of 24!"[24]

His concerns were short-lived. The British troops retreated from Norway, hoping to fight against the Germans elsewhere. A

Norwegian, watching as the last of the British soldiers withdrew on April 30, quipped, "It looks as if the British are going to fight to the last Norwegian."[25]

✳ ✳ ✳

Prime Minister Chamberlain faced Parliament on May 7, 1940, amid shouts for his resignation. The failure of the British Expeditionary Forces in Norway was an unforgivable humiliation. Apart from praising the bravery of the soldiers, Chamberlain could say little—though that didn't stop him from speaking for fifty-seven minutes.[26]

Chamberlain's support in the government hemorrhaged away. One member of Parliament echoed the words of Oliver Cromwell when he dismissed the Long Parliament in 1653: "You have sat here too long for any good you have been doing. Depart, I say—let us have done with you. In the name of God, go!"[27]

✳ ✳ ✳

Warnie Lewis spent part of the spring in a military hospital. Though it's unclear what afflicted him, some biographers have speculated that he'd been binge drinking.

Jack, always anxious about his brother's health, expressed the sentiment to Warnie that it would be far better—and less expensive—for the military to allow him to recuperate in England rather than a foreign hospital. Warnie recovered and was returned to duty with a promise of leave.

Communicating by post was a frustration for the brothers. By March 17, 1940, Jack guessed that four letters from him had been undelivered and were now chasing Warnie around France or "rotting in some empty office." It was a nuisance and reminded Jack of "the sensation of conversing with a deaf man!"[28]

Adding to his anxiety, Jack often found himself frustrated, if not bewildered, by the ongoing conflicts and dramas between the women at The Kilns. Mrs. Moore argued with her daughter or the maids, or she was in a state about the evacuees or suffering from a bout of rheumatism.

In a wry admission, Jack acknowledged that war seemed more remote from the college than The Kilns, in part because of the civilized environment at the college, but more because of the "superiority of any male society" over the chaos of his household.[29]

Relief came early in May when Warnie arrived in Oxford. Not only was he on leave, but he'd been evacuated from France to Wales with his entire unit. Jack described Warnie's presence as "a breath of fresh air."[30] Warnie, for his part, was optimistic about the outcome of the war.

After several days Warnie rejoined his unit at Wenvoe Camp in Cardiff, Wales. And just in time. All hell broke loose in Europe.

❋ ❋ ❋

The German military, emboldened by its successes in Denmark and Norway, invaded Holland and Belgium early on May 10, 1940.

By then, Prime Minister Chamberlain had announced his resignation. Winston Churchill was chosen as prime minister and given the task of forming a new administration to lead the war effort.

The armies of Great Britain and France raced northeastward to Belgium to waylay the Germans. Though the armies were evenly matched, the Germans had the advantage of a unified command, whereas the British, French, Dutch, and Belgians were uncoordinated (in part because the Dutch and Belgians refused to prepare for war in the name of neutrality). Allied leaders were confounded. There was no stopping the German juggernaut.

WINSTON CHURCHILL

By the time he became prime minister in 1940, Winston Churchill (1874–1965) was in his midsixties, had fought as an officer in two major military conflicts and two wars, and was an established politician, writer, historian, and artist. He had been a solitary voice against the rise of Nazi Germany's military efforts in the 1930s.

The son of Lord Randolph Churchill, a direct descendant of the first duke of Marlborough, and Jennie Jerome, the daughter of an American publisher, Churchill established himself as a young officer in the army and a newspaper correspondent, reporting from India and the Boer War. He won a seat in the House of Commons in 1900, where he served, with brief interruptions, for more than sixty years. He held a variety of positions in the government, including services as first lord of the admiralty, secretary of state for war, and, ultimately, prime minister. He was considered too unpredictable by both conservatives and liberals as he championed social reform and military strength. He was outspoken against Soviet Bolshevism and the appeasement of Hitler, whom he considered truly evil.

When he wasn't engaged in politics, Churchill wrote biographies, histories, and memoirs; the apex of his literary efforts was reached in 1953 when he won the Nobel Prize. Upon his death in 1965, Queen Elizabeth II gave him the rare honor of a State funeral. The world mourned.[31]

In only five days, the Dutch surrendered and the Germans broke through the Allied lines in northern France. Paul Reynaud, the French premier, phoned the newly installed Winston Churchill and cried, "We have been defeated! We are beaten!"[32]

The British Expeditionary Force, along with French and Belgian troops, were ill-equipped to fight the modern German weaponry. One French general proclaimed, "This war is sheer madness. We have gone to war with a 1918 army against a German Army of 1939."[33]

German armored columns struck southward into France through the valley of the Somme, capturing the city of Amiens. Then they pushed southwest to Boulogne, effectively cutting off the northern coastal towns of France from the rest of the country.

More than three hundred thousand Allied troops were trapped in France at Dunkirk, a coastal town near the border of Belgium.[34] The Germans were in sight of it, ready to destroy what was left of the Allied forces, when an overconfident Hitler told his army to wait. The British had their backs against the sea and weren't going anywhere, Hitler assumed. Surely they had the good sense to surrender. Against protests from his military advisors, Hitler ordered the German army to move south, deeper into France, and on to Paris. The Luftwaffe, meanwhile, were tasked with regular attacks on the stranded troops.

Hitler underestimated the fortitude of a sea-faring nation like Great Britain. In a dramatic rescue effort that lasted from May 26 until June 4, 1940, more than nine hundred merchant-marine vessels, fishing boats, and pleasure boats—almost anything seaworthy—left England to join British naval ships in evacuating the Allied forces from France.[35] The civilian craft ventured into an inferno from two million tons of oil that had poured into the channel from the port's tanks.[36] The air stank of smoke and putrid flesh. Men, stretched along the twenty miles of beach, saw the boats, and many plunged into the water in full gear, only to disappear beneath the waves.

More than ten thousand men were killed or missing. Forty thousand had been taken prisoner. But over three hundred thirty thousand men were rescued.[37]

It was the "miracle" of Dunkirk.

✳ ✳ ✳

On June 4, 1940, Prime Minister Winston Churchill told Parliament and the British people,

> Even though large tracts of Europe and many old and famous States have fallen or may fall into the grip of the Gestapo and all the odious apparatus of Nazi rule, we shall not flag or fail. We shall go on to the end, we shall fight in France, we shall fight on the seas and oceans, we shall fight with growing confidence and growing strength in the air, we shall defend our Island, whatever the cost may be, we shall fight on the beaches, we shall fight on the landing grounds, we shall fight in the fields and in the streets, we shall fight in the hills; we shall never surrender.[38]

Mary Shearburn, Churchill's secretary, recalled how Churchill had wept while dictating the speech to her two nights before it was delivered to the nation.[39]

✳ ✳ ✳

The Belgian army fought hard but surrendered on May 28, 1940. On June 10, Italy declared war on Britain and France. Within five days, German troops entered Paris. Within eight days after that, the French signed an armistice with Hitler himself—in the same railroad car in Compiègne where Germany had capitulated to France in 1918.

※ ※ ※

"What General Weygand [has] called the Battle of France is over," Churchill announced on June 18, 1940:

> I expect that the Battle of Britain is about to begin. Upon
> this battle depends the survival of Christian civilization. . . .
> The whole fury and might of the enemy must very soon
> be turned on us. Hitler knows that he will have to break
> us in this Island or lose the war. . . . Let us therefore brace
> ourselves to our duties, and so bear ourselves that, if the
> British Empire and its Commonwealth last for a thousand
> years, men will still say, "This was their finest hour."[40]

※ ※ ※

The first bombs fell on the British mainland near Canterbury on May 9, 1940. Middlesbrough was the first industrial city to be attacked on May 24. One day after the French surrendered to Germany on June 18, bombs fell on London, hitting plough land at Addington in Surrey.[41]

These incidents were only a foretaste of what would come.

※ ※ ※

On a Friday evening in July 1940, Jack and his good friend Humphrey Havard listened to Hitler on the radio. Jack later mused that while the speech lasted, it was hard not to believe what Hitler was saying. He marveled how statements he knew to be lies sounded convincingly true as long as they were spoken "unflinchingly."[42]

Not long after that, an idea came to Jack about devils. He'd been sick for a while and finally felt well enough to go to church.

Maybe it was the sermon, which he didn't consider very good, but Jack had an idea for a book that he thought might be both "useful and entertaining." The title he entertained was *As One Devil to Another*. It would be a compilation of letters from "an elderly retired devil to a young devil who has just started work on his first 'patient.'"[43]

The inspiration struck him so powerfully that he began to work out the details. The letters he wrote to Warnie would explore "the psychology of temptation" from a diabolical point of view.[44] He even presented a sample, sketching out a few thoughts about prayer and faith. The devil would reference God as "the Enemy," and so on.

Jack was describing what would eventually comprise the second and twenty-seventh letters from *The Screwtape Letters*.

✳ ✳ ✳

Meanwhile, in the real world, diabolical forces went to work.

Germany's military strategists convinced Hitler that they had to gain superiority over the coastal towns and the skies of England before they could implement Operation Sea Lion, Hitler's plan to invade Britain. Positioning itself from captured airfields in France and Belgium, the Luftwaffe was unleashed. The Battle of Britain began.

The first wave of attacks hit British convoys in the English Channel and the ports of southeast England on July 10, 1940. The plan was to draw out the Royal Air Force to be destroyed. The British pilots, with odds-defying luck and determination, repulsed the superior German air force.

In August, the Germans then focused their attention on the RAF itself, engaging in dogfights over Britain. On most days the RAF was outnumbered three to one. Even as the number of

British planes increased from production, the number of pilots didn't. Inadequately trained and unskilled, those who didn't die in the day-to-day dogfights were physically and emotionally exhausted, living on three hours of sleep a night and fighting in the air far longer than most pilots were capable of handling under normal conditions. Yet the RAF not only held its own but also prevailed against the Luftwaffe. German aircraft, which were considered unbeatable only a few months before, suddenly met their match with the British Spitfires and Hurricanes.

On August 20, Churchill paid the RAF pilots tribute in the House of Commons, proclaiming, "Never in the field of human conflict was so much owed by so many to so few."[45]

Members of the German high command puzzled over the Luftwaffe's inability to master their enemy. They argued over the deficiencies of the aircraft they'd been using. The short-range fighters were quickly in trouble because of the fuel they had to use just to cross the channel, let alone fight for any length of time over Britain. Daylight raids saw the German air force losing significantly more planes than the British. The case was made that night raids on London would draw out the RAF to a single area—allowing for a greater chance to destroy them—and the British people would be demoralized by the inevitable death and destruction. Yet before any decision was made, an accident happened that determined the course of events.

On the night of August 24, 1940, 170 German bombers flew to attack oil and aircraft plants from Kent in the south of England and as far north as Scotland. Two of the pilots got lost. The British hit them with a barrage of anti-aircraft fire from the ground. The pilots decided to abandon the mission. They dropped their payloads and headed east to escape.

What the pilots didn't know was that they had dropped their

payloads on London itself, the first bombs to hit the city since 1918. St. Giles Church in Cripplegate was destroyed. In other areas, people coming out of pubs and cinemas were killed in the streets. The first blood from civilians in nonmilitary areas had been spilled.[46]

Though it was clear the bombings were unintentional, Churchill retaliated with air assaults on Berlin, causing little damage but killing the first Berliner by a British bomb. The psychological effect was devastating. Hermann Goering, who had promised Berliners they would never suffer such a breech, was enraged.[47]

On September 4, Hitler gave a speech in Berlin to promote the winter wartime effort to an assembly of Berlin's social workers and nurses. He took the opportunity to address the attacks by calling the British cowards for coming over only at night, while the German air force attacked during the day. (Of course, he didn't explain that the German bases in France and Belgium made that possible for the Germans, whereas it was far more difficult for the British to fly all the way to Germany from England.)

"When they declare that they will increase their attacks on our cities," Hitler railed, "then we will raze *their* cities to the ground. We will stop the handiwork of these air pirates, so help us God."

He paused in his speech to allow for the wild applause.

"And when the British air force drops two or three or four thousand kilograms of bombs, then we will in one night drop 150-, 230-, 300-, or 400,000 kilograms," he exclaimed.[48]

The audience leaped to their feet in hysteria.

Hitler basked in it. "In England they're filled with curiosity and keep asking: 'Why doesn't he come?' Be calm. . . . He's coming! He's coming!"

More laughter and wild applause.

"The hour will come when one of us will break," Hitler concluded, "and it will not be National Socialist Germany."[49]

The blitzkrieg would soon begin.

THE BLITZ

FOR THE FIRST TIME IN more than twenty years, Jack put on a uniform. And he found it incomprehensible to assemble. The straps, loops, and buttons confused him. He would have preferred to stay in his normal clothes. But as a member of Oxford's Local Defence Volunteers, he was expected to look the part. The overall effect wasn't impressive. "As I look in the glass, it's one to a million that any civilian will look [like] such an absolute ass," he wrote to his brother.[1]

The arrival of a uniform he hadn't requested may have reminded Jack of his time in the trenches of France. One day, guns no one had ordered suddenly appeared: it meant they were about to engage the enemy.

Churchill had warned the nation that, having conquered much of Europe, Hitler would turn his eye to Britain. Rumors of an imminent German invasion became commonplace. The Battle of Britain raged overhead with the Luftwaffe trying unsuccessfully to destroy the RAF. Nerves were on edge as the average citizen anticipated spies, saboteurs, and soldiers parachuting into their gardens in the still of the night.

One evening Mrs. Moore heard footsteps outside The Kilns.

Believing that German paratroopers had landed, she rushed out to confront them. Instead of the enemy, however, she encountered two British soldiers taking a shortcut through the property. She then discovered they were from Northern Ireland and invited them into the kitchen for bottles of stout. Jack was later amused when "their old world courtesy" prompted the soldiers to return the next night for more of the same kind of hospitality.[2]

In the midst of the international conflict and anxiety about Germany's next move, normal life pressed on. August 1940 brought two domestic changes. Mrs. Moore's daughter, Maureen, became engaged. And Warren Lewis, now a major, officially retired from the army.

The former change meant that The Kilns's household would become absorbed in wedding plans. Jack would bear the brunt of the financial obligations for the bride-to-be and suffer the additional chaos with a smile.

The latter change was a relief to Jack. Warnie's retirement meant he was home for good; his intention was to serve privately with the Oxford City Home Guard Battalion and captain his boat, the *Bosphorus*,[3] as part of his duties in the Upper Thames River Patrol. He even took to wearing a blue-peaked navy cap and painted the boat battleship-gray.[4]

Why Warnie retired when, in theory, his military experience should have been needed in the war effort is a mystery. Biographers could find nothing in his discharge papers to suggest a reason. Warnie never talked about his experiences in the Second World War, prompting George Sayer to conclude Warnie felt "deep shame."[5] Sayer assumed that Warnie had been drinking heavily throughout this period, which led to his frequent visits to the hospital.

Whatever the reason, Jack was glad to have Warnie home.

Mrs. Moore, on the other hand, couldn't have been pleased. In his memoirs, Warnie would later write about her resentment over any time Jack spent away from her, and the constant burdens she placed on Jack when he was around. For her part, Mrs. Moore may have felt that Warnie's alcoholism was the *real* burden for Jack.

There is no record that Mrs. Moore and Warnie ever spoke of how they felt about each other. They restrained their antipathy for Jack's sake. When things got particularly tense, Warnie retreated to the *Bosphorus*.

The changes to life at The Kilns was a hint of greater changes to come.

✳ ✳ ✳

James Welch and Eric Fenn were frustrated with the state of the BBC's religious broadcasting. The acceleration of the war meant little could be accomplished to push their programming to the next level. Innovations in religious broadcasting weren't a priority when the nation was hanging on to survival by its fingernails. So the old standbys of religious services continued throughout the week.

Welch hadn't given up, though. He remained convinced that his department could do more to speak into the lives of the BBC's listeners. As a relatively easy next step, he looked to a mainstay of British programming: broadcast talks. These were relatively short programs—ten to twenty minutes—intended to appeal directly to the listeners' war-time needs. And they became extremely popular.

Cecil Henry Middleton, an expert in gardening, took fifteen minutes with *In Your Garden* to give listeners tips and advice about flowers, weeds, bushes, and general horticultural concerns.

Later, when the government launched its Dig for Victory initiative to inspire the British population to grow their own food, Middleton talked everyone through the ups and downs of planting and harvesting. Audiences were charmed by his plainspoken common sense and gentle humor.

If listeners weren't sure what to do with the food they had been rationed or had grown, the daily five-minute *Kitchen Front* helped them along. Featuring Gert and Daisy (stage names for Elsie and Doris Waters), the cantankerous Grandma Buggins (Mabel Constanduros), and host Freddy Grisewood (sometimes known as "Ricepud"), listeners were told how to make the most of carrots, parsnips, potatoes, elderberries, and even prunes. The show was good-natured, fun, packed with horrible puns, and of greater importance, practical.[6]

With gardening and food came the need for the *Radio Doctor*. Presented anonymously by Dr. Charles Hill, the secretary of the British Medical Association, the show offered helpful medical advice and often talked about things never allowed in other BBC programs—bowel movements, for example. Hill often praised "that humble black-coated worker, the prune" in his ongoing fight against the nation's constipation. He once described a pathologist as "a man who sits on one stool and examines those of other people." As for regularity, he encouraged listeners to "visit the throne at the same time each day, whether you feel like it or not."[7]

Beyond providing practical helps, commentators were regularly heard on programs like *Postscripts*. Speakers included actors Robert Donat, Leslie Howard, Duff Cooper, and even the American journalist Quentin Reynolds. By far the most popular commentator was novelist J. B. Priestley. Priestley, a robust Yorkshireman, articulated the heart of the nation with his insightful views and compelling prose. Popular singer Vera Lynn observed that "while Churchill rallied the nation with stirring images from [the past], Priestley concentrated" on familiar images of the present: a night spent with a Home Guard unit, a drunken man singing in an air-raid shelter, or an off-season visit to a seaside resort. Listeners readily embraced Priestley as one of their family.[8]

For Welch, the common denominator of these successful programs was a voice that exuded warmth, common sense, inspiration, humor, and humanity. If subjects such as gardening and bodily functions could have those kinds of champions, why not religion?

Writing in the 1942 edition of *The BBC Handbook*, Welch stated,

> In a time of uncertainty and questioning it is the responsibility of the Church—and of religious broadcasting as one of its most powerful voices—to declare the truth about God and His relation to men. It has to expound the Christian faith in terms that can be easily understood by ordinary men and women, and to examine ways in which that faith can be applied to present-day society during these difficult times.[9]

Now all he had to do was find the voice to pull off such a feat.

❋ ❋ ❋

Around 4:30 p.m. on September 7, 1940, just a little over a year after war had been declared, more than 350 bombers, with more than 600 fighters to escort them, flew up the Thames Estuary.[10]

Any assumption that this was yet another attack on RAF bases was quickly dispelled as the planes pressed on to London. England had never seen so many bombers. Witnesses who watched the breathtaking spectacle wondered why the RAF didn't engage the invaders. What they couldn't know was that the RAF Fighter Command purposefully held back its pilots; to engage would have been a massacre.

Within an hour, it looked as if Hitler's vow to break Great Britain was being fulfilled: the East End of London was being razed to the ground. Londoners, viewing the nightmare, thought the world was ending.

The German planes moved off, and the all clear sounded around 6:10 p.m. In just under two hours, the Germans had attacked both industrial and residential areas. Stunned survivors emerged from the shelters to a scene of hellish devastation. Fires raged, buildings fell. The dead were strewn about, the injured cried out from the rubble.

The fire brigades and emergency service personnel were overwhelmed as the blazes burned out of control. Gas mains exploded. Rescue operations were ineffective and chaotic. Debris filled the roads, blocking ambulances and fire apparatus. Few could get in or out of the damaged areas. The communications infrastructure was disabled. All of the government's preparations and plans fell apart in the onslaught.

The people of London, shocked and confused, sought help and searched for loved ones. The extent of the damage—the sheer apocalypse of fire, smoke, and ruin—was more than most could ever have imagined. They had no idea it was only the beginning. Within two hours, the air-raid sirens wailed again.

Using the fires of the East End to guide them, nearly 250

bombers returned to London. Squadrons of Heinkels and Dorniers came, wave after wave, to bring hell upon the city. Tons of high-explosive bombs and incendiary canisters screamed toward the city below. Parachutes carrying land mines packed with a ton of high explosives floated down. Upon impact, there was a blinding flash of pink light and then a blast that reduced entire streets and all upon them to flame and dust.[11]

If there were specific targets for the German pilots, no one on the ground knew what they were. As far as anyone could tell, all of London was the target.

By 3:00 a.m., the raid had reached its peak. The stores of the East End warehouses were destroyed. Industrial cranes buckled and fell over onto emergency rescue personnel. Paint, rubber, tea, sugar, and wheat—precious rations—fed the flames. Nearly a million tons of softwood were destroyed. Firefighters could hardly breathe from the toxic fumes. The fires grew so intense that the water used to fight them turned instantly to steam. The paint on fireboats sitting more than three hundred yards away blistered.[12]

ARP wardens, who for months had paraded about in their uniforms with their whistle blowing and superior posturing, came undone. Some cowered and some ran away, never to be seen again. Others fought bravely, against all odds.

In the shelters, people knelt and cried. Others defied the catastrophe by conducting publike sing-alongs.

By the time the all clear sounded at five o'clock the next morning, some 430 people had been killed, and around 1,600 seriously injured. More than one thousand fires had been reported.[13]

And Hitler was not finished. For the next fifty-six nights, the German bombers came.

✳ ✳ ✳

With the declaration of war in 1939, the BBC's Broadcasting House took precautions. Stacks of sandbags protected the entrance. More were strategically placed around its shiplike perimeter. Antigas doors were installed. The police were assigned to guard the building around the clock to prevent any sabotage by so-called fifth columnists and subversives.

With the start of the Battle of Britain during the summer, soldiers replaced the police outside, and Local Defense Volunteers patrolled inside. A wire-and-steel pillbox was placed in front of the main doors. Concrete blocks were added to the sandbags. In case Broadcasting House itself was destroyed, a concrete bunker at one end of the building contained a complete broadcasting station with all the studios, rooms, and transmitters needed to keep the BBC operating.

On October 15, 1940, a five-hundred-pound, delayed-action bomb crashed through a seventh-floor window. It smashed through four floors until it came to rest in the music library, which was in the center of the building. The damage and noise were so extensive that some of the staff didn't realize the bomb hadn't actually exploded.

A concerned employee, believing the bomb could detonate at any time and do worse damage to the building, tried to move the bomb to an outer hall. The bomb went off, killing seven people.

In the basement studio, Bruce Belfrage was reading the nine o'clock news when the bomb exploded. He paused only long enough for the plaster to stop falling on him and then calmly said it was all right. He continued, making only one slight mistake as he introduced the next program.[14]

THE TOP HAT SCHEME

Broadcasting House, the home of the BBC, was designed in an art-deco style by architect Col. Val Myer and was built in 1932. Nicknamed the Top Hat scheme, the original design was based on the American skyscraper and centered around a studio tower to be flanked by offices, allowing in daylight. Local residents complained about having such a tall building dwarfing their homes in shadow, so the design was redone, giving the new version an asymmetrical form in which one side of the top was lower than the other.

By the time Broadcasting House was completed, it seemed to resemble a large ship sailing down Great Portland Street for Oxford Circus. Reactions to the design were mixed. The *Architectural Review* of 1932 proclaimed it the new Tower of London, while admitting it was clearly "a struggle between moribund traditionalism and inventive modernism." One critic called it "that petrified dreadnought."[15] Over the years the building has become an iconic fixture in London.

Dedicated to "Almighty God" as a "Temple of Arts and Muses"—according to the Latin inscription in the entrance hall—the building was one of the first in the world constructed solely for broadcasting purposes (coming after Berlin's Radio Center and New York's Radio City).

Studios, the news library, the record library, and the main switchboard were destroyed.

Damage wasn't limited to just Broadcasting House but extended to the Langham Hotel across the street. Upper rooms were blown to the pavement below. The remains of a London bus were found hanging precariously on a nearby roof.

Less than two months later, on December 8, 1940, a parachute-delivered landmine fell and exploded on Great Portland Street. A policeman was instantly killed, and the side of Broadcasting House destroyed. Fire broke out inside the building and burned uncontrolled for seven hours. Ironically, much of the damage came from broken water pipes and fire hoses that turned staircases into waterfalls, flooding the entrance hall and the newsroom.

In a testimony to their dedication, the kitchen staff, choked and flooded, still prepared five hundred breakfasts for employees and emergency personnel the next morning.[16]

✳ ✳ ✳

Though the people of Oxford didn't suffer German bombings, the impact of the Blitz in London affected them deeply. Everyone knew someone who had been hurt or killed. Families were displaced from their bombed-out homes. The Kilns still welcomed evacuee children three at a time.

As in any crisis, people's spiritual sensibilities were sharpened as they came face-to-face with death. Eternal questions, long forgotten in times of peace, came back to mind.

In October, Jack took the unusual step of going to an Anglican priest for confession. It was unusual because the act of confession wasn't common in the Church of England nor, for that matter, in Jack's experience. Yet he felt compelled to do it. "The *decision* to do so was one of the hardest I have ever made," he wrote to a friend, "but now . . . I am committed (by dint of posting the letter before I had time to change my mind)." Jack questioned his motives, wondering if he was merely indulging in an "orgy of egoism." He found the thought of confession both "terrifying" and a "wonderful opportunity."[17] Eventually he found peace by thinking of a quote that guided so much of his work and attitude about the faith: "Let us hold on to that which has been believed everywhere, always, by everyone."[18] Confession was one of those things worth holding on to.

Jack made his confession to Father Walter Adams, a member of the Society of Saint John the Evangelist, an Anglican religious community. He struggled with Father Adams being "much too close to Rome" and made it clear he couldn't follow the priest "in certain directions."[19] On the other hand, Father Adams impressed Jack with his understanding of the human soul. "If I have ever met a *holy* man, he is one," Jack stated.[20]

Though Jack called the experience a "wall of fire," he discovered, to his surprise, that he was agreeable to doing it again. He attributed his worries about confession being "an orgy of egoism" to "enemy propaganda"—which always has a "grain of truth" but shouldn't stop us from doing the right thing. "For after all everything—even virtue, even prayer—has its dangers," he concluded, "and if one heeds the grain of truth in the enemy propaganda one can never do anything at all."[21]

In those words we get a glimpse of his thinking behind *The Screwtape Letters*. He later admitted that writing *Screwtape* was hard on him spiritually because he had to get into the mind of a demon to do the job properly. "Beauty, freshness, and geniality" were gone. It was all "dust, grit, thirst, and itch," which nearly "smothered" him.[22]

Little wonder he decided to find a confessor. He continued the practice throughout the rest of his life.

The Success of *Screwtape*

Jack subscribed to only one periodical—the *Guardian*—a weekly Anglican newspaper. He had already written one essay for it called "Dangers of National Repentance" and would soon write a second titled "Two Ways with the Self."[23] Jack finished *The Screwtape Letters* by the end of 1940 and offered them to the editor. The editor wisely agreed. The first letter from Screwtape premiered on Friday, May 2, 1941.

In no time at all, *The Screwtape Letters* became a great success. The senior demon's relationship with his nephew Wormwood, the life of the "patient" and his various relationships, a romance, the backdrop of the war, and the ongoing twists and turns of temptation took on a soap-opera-like quality. Subscriptions for the *Guardian* increased, and nonsubscribers sought out the newspaper if only to read what would happen.

Ashley Sampson, the editor who had commissioned *The Problem of Pain*, suggested to publisher Geoffrey Bles that he ought to publish *The Screwtape Letters*. Bles met with Jack, forming a publishing relationship that would last for decades. Jack wrote a brief introduction to the completed collection, and it arrived in the bookstores on February 9, 1942.[24] Macmillan published the work in the United States a year later.[25]

✳ ✳ ✳

Whether it was intentional or not, *Screwtape* reflected another part of Jack's life: his relationship with Mrs. Moore. In the letters, the "patient"—the human under attack by Screwtape's nephew—has a domineering mother whose love is almost tyrannical. Screwtape teaches his nephew how to exploit the relationship through the "daily pinpricks" between mother and son, and resentment over the "patient's" conversion in Letter 3, her alarm over his faith in Letter 10, the "gluttony of Delicacy" in Letter 17, and the scathingly funny "Generous Conflict Illusion" in Letter 26.[26] These situations ring true for many families, but they contain a specificity that could easily point to Jack's relationship with Mrs. Moore.

❋ ❋ ❋

The Problem of Pain was published on October 18, 1940. The reviews were strong. The *Church Times* praised Jack for his "clarity" and his ability to "sympathize with the difficulties of the average man who is troubled by doubts." A reviewer in the *Guardian* commended his "sound scholarship" and his "frank admission of mysteries and unpalatable facts."[27]

The book had its detractors as well. Evelyn Underhill, an Anglo-Catholic proponent of Christian mysticism, privately took issue with the chapter "Animal Pain." Various members of the clergy also challenged him on specific statements in the book. Jack, who felt duty bound to answer every letter, got his first glimpse of the work and time he'd have to spend as a popular author on correspondence.

Even Jack's good friend Charles Williams jabbed at him. In a discussion about the biblical character of Job, Williams wryly observed that God didn't direct His displeasure at the weak and impatient Job but at those who presumed to be "comforters," the "self-appointed advocates on God's side" who claimed that "all was well." "The sort of people," Williams said, looking directly at Jack, "who wrote books on the Problem of Pain."[28]

However, Williams's jab didn't prevent him from reviewing

the book in *Theology* magazine (January 1941) and commending Jack's style as "goodness working on goodness, a lucid and sincere intellect at work on the facts of life."[29]

J. R. R. Tolkien had his own issues with Jack's work. According to Colin Duriez in *Tolkien and C. S. Lewis: The Gift of Friendship*, Tolkien "strongly disapproved" of laypeople tackling theological matters, believing such matters were better left to professional clergy. It bothered him enough that years later he wrote a letter praising the work of theologian Austin Farrer, stating that if real theologians like Farrer had written theology for laypeople sooner "'the world would have been spared' C. S. Lewis."[30]

Duriez is quick to point out that the conflict was never personal but simply one of *approach*: Tolkien held the view that a more allusive approach to the Christian faith through story and imaginative writings was best—and, as a result, he lauded Lewis's *The Great Divorce* and *Perelandra*. Jack, on the other hand, employed many approaches to his fiction and nonfiction writings. The disagreement didn't impair their friendship. Tolkien, as a member of the Inklings, often heard and commented on Jack's theological works before they were published.

Ironically, the one book by Jack that effectively blended Tolkien's approach with imagination and Jack's overt exploration of theology was *The Screwtape Letters*. Jack dedicated it to Tolkien.

* * *

It is a small but significant note that *The Problem of Pain* cut across most denominational lines. Jack was able to deal with his subject without alienating any particular branch of Christianity.

In his preface to the French edition, Jack explained that before he became a Christian, he perceived something that those brought up in the church might miss: in spite of the church's divisions, there was still an essential unity. "Even when I feared and detested Christianity . . . I trembled on recognizing the same unmistakable aroma coming from the writings of Dante and Bunyan, Thomas Aquinas and William Law."[31]

It was Jack's ability to communicate nondenominationally to a broad audience that led him to a new chapter in his life.

✳ ✳ ✳

James Welch was still searching for a particular kind of "voice" to herald in a new approach to religious broadcasting at the BBC. He hoped to find someone accessible, insightful, and inspiring to give faith a fresh relevancy to their listeners. But *where* would he find someone like that?

Then Welch read *The Problem of Pain*.

8

CONVERGENCE

"BY THE GOODNESS OF GOD we mean nowadays almost exclusively His lovingness," Jack wrote in *The Problem of Pain*:

> "And by Love, in this context, most of us mean kindness—the desire to see others than the self happy; not happy in this way or in that, but just happy. What would really satisfy us would be a God who said of anything we happened to like doing, "What does it matter so long as they are contented?" We want, in fact, not so much a Father in Heaven as a grandfather in heaven—a senile benevolence who, as they say, "liked to see young people enjoying themselves" and whose plan for the universe was simply that it might be truly said at the end of each day, 'a good time was had by all."[1]

James Welch was deeply impressed by the way Jack had dealt with such a difficult topic. In *The Problem of Pain* he found the tone, common sense, and insights he needed for the BBC's religious programming.

On February 7, 1941, Welch wrote to Jack to express how

grateful he was for *The Problem of Pain* and "the help this book has given me." He ventured to ask if Jack would be willing to help the BBC with religious broadcasting. "The microphone is a limiting, and often irritating, instrument, but the quality of thinking and the depth of conviction which I find in your book ought surely to be shared with a great many other people."[2]

Hoping for a yes from Jack, he suggested two ideas they might consider. One would explore "the Christian, or lack of Christian, assumptions underlying modern literature."[3] The second was a layperson's look at the Christian faith, articulating core Christian ideas so the average person could understand them. If Jack was agreeable, Eric Fenn would be in touch.

Jack disliked the radio, finding it annoying and intrusive, much as he would detest television later.[4] However, he responded three days later with the yes Welch wanted. He agreed to give a series of talks but, no, not on modern literature. He counterproposed a series on "the Law of Nature," or objective right and wrong. His rationale was that ideas of repentance and forgiveness were lost on most people because they'd lost their understanding of why they needed to repent or be forgiven—they'd lost their sense of guilt and needed to get it back. He wouldn't mention Christianity until the end. He also suggested a title like *The Art of Being Shocked* or *These Humans* as a possibility.

If any of these ideas were acceptable, Jack wrote, he could do the broadcasts during his break from Magdalen College in August.

As Welch promised, Eric Fenn took the lead and wrote to Jack to ask for about four twenty-minute talks in August or September. Jack agreed and invited Fenn to Oxford for lunch. It was April before the two men met face-to-face.

Welch and Fenn weren't without their misgivings about the

gamble they were taking. And, no doubt, it *was* a gamble. Jack Lewis might have been a gifted writer and lecturer, but his style and voice might not work well on a national radio broadcast.

How could they prepare him for the realities of broadcasting—the script revisions, rehearsals, timing, and vocal style? Could they coach him properly to speak to the masses within the parameters of radio—and would he agree?

Unbeknownst to Welch and Fenn, an opportunity presented itself to Jack that helped address their concerns.

* * *

On a rainy night during February 1941, the RAF's chaplain in chief, Maurice Edwards, and a young advisor named Reverend Charles Gilmore paid a visit to Jack in his rooms at Magdalen College. Edwards, an Anglican clergyman in his midfifties, had written to Jack about meeting to discuss the possibility of lecturing to the young men and women in the RAF around Great Britain.

Jack, who had originally suggested this sort of idea to President George Gordon at the beginning of the war, agreed to meet.

Edwards was confident that Jack was the right man for the job. After all, the dean of St. Paul's Cathedral had personally recommended him, having read Jack's work. Charles Gilmore, on the other hand, wasn't so sure.

As a man of modest education and academic achievement, Gilmore wondered if Jack—a "teacher's teacher"—could talk to an audience of "civilians in uniform" who weren't academics, nor aspired to be, but wanted answers *if* they survived to see the "postwar world."[5]

Jack was interested but hesitant. He shared Gilmore's concerns about his ability to speak to that audience. It was one thing to lecture cadets attending Oxford, but this was a greater challenge.

Whatever reservations he had, Jack wasn't one to allow them to get in the way of an opportunity to help others through his teaching. It wasn't ego, or any pleasure he received from hearing his own voice, but a candid assessment of his strengths and weaknesses. He believed that if he was a good teacher, then it was a matter of duty, before God, to teach. So, yes, he would do it.

His first presentation would be in April, at the RAF Bomber Command in Abingdon, about five miles from Oxford.

✳ ✳ ✳

On March 16 and 17, 1941, 108 German bombers[6] made a concentrated night attack on Bristol.

Welch, who was hosting the *Postscripts* program, had to relocate to a small emergency studio—too small to accommodate the assembled orchestra. So, as the bombs fell, Welch did his talk from underneath a table, with announcer Stuart Hibberd reading the Bible next to him and a single violinist, Paul Beard, playing the violin on his knees.

The residential areas around the city took the brunt of the bombs, with the industrial and dockland areas left mostly undamaged. Initial reports put the death toll at 208.[7]

Welch was glad he'd had the experience, since it allowed him to understand firsthand what many in his audience had been suffering. Welch's empathy—his desire to connect to his listeners—was paramount to his work.

Two of the three major studios were destroyed, and the BBC decided it was time for the Religious Broadcasting department to relocate to a safer region. Bedford, sixty miles north of London, was chosen for its lack of factories to attract the German air force. A local hotel would provide rooms as offices, while worship services would be broadcast from the parish church and a nearby chapel. The Corn Exchange, a large hall, was chosen for concerts. Appropriately, it was in Bedford that John Bunyan was jailed for twelve years and wrote the classic *The Pilgrim's Progress*.

The move would take place during the summer, adding one more complexity to Fenn's work and his communication with Jack.

After the announcement was made about Welch's department moving away, a local newspaper declared, "Religion leaving Bristol."[8]

* * *

Jack was not only a reader of the *Guardian*, but he also contributed articles and essays. Jack offered *The Screwtape Letters* to the editor, believing the format was ideal for serialization. The editor was delighted and offered Jack two pounds for each letter. (From this time forward, Jack would donate the money from this kind of work to those in need.) The first "Screwtape" letter appeared in the newspaper on May 2, 1941, and an installment was featured weekly for the next thirty-one weeks.

The letters from the devil Screwtape were a huge success. Jack's insights about humanity, temptation, rationalization, and the endless maneuvering of demonic powers with human weakness proved irresistible to readers. The newspaper's subscriptions rose to new heights as people wanted to read the next installment.

If the mail from *The Problem of Pain* placed a burden on Jack, then the mail generated by *Screwtape* nearly overwhelmed him. Readers wrote to offer their appreciation, ask questions, or argue points Jack had made.

The Demands of Wartime Letter Writing

There are multiple volumes of C. S. Lewis's published letters. He wrote diligently to family, friends, admirers, and casual inquirers. But the rationing of paper and ink during the war made his letter writing a particular challenge—exacerbated by the many letters he received after the first series of broadcasts. A look through the files of the BBC archives shows letters written on the reverse sides of correspondence he'd cut into small squares, along with other scraps and postcards. Since Jack never learned to type, everything was handwritten, putting further demands on his need for ink. In addition to all of his other duties, Jack spent hours dealing with letters.

The return of his brother from military service gave Jack a helpful reprieve as Warnie took on the job of secretary. Warnie took dictation directly from Jack or merely answered on Jack's behalf using a portable Royal typewriter.

In a diary entry from 1967, four years after Jack's death, Warnie lamented that the typewriter had broken down. He took it to a shop for repair only to find that no parts for it existed. He felt the loss, as "it has been [his] companion for thirty-five years, almost half [his] lifetime." From that typewriter he had compiled the exhaustive *Lewis Papers*, his own biographies and books, and an estimate of "at least twelve thousand of [Jack's] letters."[9]

The success of *The Screwtape Letters* also drew an offer from Ashley Sampson, the editor who had originally commissioned *The Problem of Pain*. The letters finished in the *Guardian* in November 1941, and the book was released the following February.

✳ ✳ ✳

Adolf Hitler was annoyed. The British would not be reasonable and surrender to Germany. The Blitz hadn't driven them to their knees, as he'd expected. Instead, the attacks made them more tenacious. The German air force intensified its efforts, attacking British ports and industrial cities. Bad weather during the early part of 1941 gave London a reprieve, but that changed on March 8 when 125 German aircraft dropped 130 tons of explosives and 30,000 incendiaries in a little over three hours. Over the next two months, more raids came, with the worst thus far hitting on April 16. More than 800 tons of high explosives and 150,000 incendiaries rained down for eight and a half hours that night. The number of casualties: more than eleven hundred people killed, and over twenty-two hundred injured. By the end of April, civilian deaths for the month had surpassed six thousand.[10]

On April 15, 1941, two days after Easter Sunday, Belfast, Ireland, was bombed. Jack heard through a cousin that his childhood neighborhoods had been hit. He worried about distant relatives and his close friend Arthur Greeves, to whom he wrote later.

Jack also worried about Minto, as her health was declining. The Kilns had become "a sad household."[11] Her conflicts with the housekeepers and demands upon Jack were constant, though his outside work increased. Warnie retreated to the *Bosphorus* whenever he could.

In the midst of all this, Jack had his debut at the RAF base in Abingdon. His worst fears were realized. He determined that the event was "a complete failure."[12] His only comfort was in remembering "that God used an ass to convert the prophet."[13]

Pen Pals

Jack Lewis wrote and received thousands of letters in his lifetime. In *Collected Letters*, certain names appear again and again. Among them are Arthur Greeves and Sister Penelope.[14]

Joseph Arthur Greeves (1895–1966) was born in Belfast to Irishman Joseph Greeves and American Mary Greeves. Arthur's father was head of a family business of flax spinners. The Greeves family home—called *Bernagh*—was situated directly across from the Lewis family home. Arthur's early attempts to get to know Jack and Warnie failed. Later, in April 1914, Jack was visiting his father and had been asked to slip across the street to visit Arthur, who was ill. Jack agreed. The meeting was an epiphany, which Jack recounted in *Surprised by Joy*,[15] as the two young men realized they had many mutual interests, beginning with Norse mythology.

From that beginning the two men remained close friends for the rest of Jack's life—sharing their most intimate thoughts in person and in letters, arguing about Christianity (Arthur became a Christian long before Jack) and comforting each other during life's trials. Jack stayed at *Bernagh* after his father died in 1929, wrote *The Pilgrim's Regress* there in 1932, and often returned for his holidays. In the summers of 1958 and 1959, Jack stayed with Arthur at his cottage called Silver Hill. Arthur visited Jack at The Kilns in 1961. It was the last time the two men saw each other.

Arthur had a modest education, achieved local acclaim as a gifted landscape painter, and participated in the businesses of various family members until a bad heart put an end to any consistent labor. He lived off his family wealth in County Down, near his family home, his entire life.

Sister Penelope (1890–1977) was Ruth Penelope Lawson, the

daughter of an Anglican vicar. She attended a school founded by the nineteenth-century Tractarian clergyman the Reverend William John Butler. Butler, along with John Henry Newman and several other writers and preachers, promoted a return of Anglicanism to an essential form of Catholicism. From these efforts, Butler founded the first Anglican religious order since the Reformation: the Community of St. Mary the Virgin, Wantage.

Sister Penelope entered the convent in 1912 and, in the ensuing years, published a variety of books on the Christian faith and used her knowledge of Greek and Latin to translate the works of the church fathers. Jack Lewis, with whom she became a correspondent in 1939 because of his novel *Out of the Silent Planet*, wrote the introduction to her translation of a work by Saint Athanasius (1953).

It wasn't until 1942 that Jack met Sister Penelope in person, after he agreed to address the junior sisters in Wantage. He would later dedicate the novel *Perelandra* to them. And, remarkably, it was to Sister Penelope that Jack entrusted his original manuscript of *The Screwtape Letters*, fearing that it might be destroyed by German bombs if he sent it to his publisher.

Some of Jack Lewis's most personal observations about his spiritual life and experiences can be found in his letters to Sister Penelope.

Reverend Charles Gilmore, who had attended in his capacity as an advisor, thought the event wasn't a complete failure. But he knew Jack needed to work on his subject matter. "To these men, probing life in the raw and trying to do something about it,"

Gilmore later wrote about one of Jack's lectures, "[Jack] chose to speak on 'Linguistic Analysis in Pauline Soteriology.'"[16]

During one lecture, an officer busied himself with the *Times* crossword. The audience fidgeted and coughed. Uncharacteristically, Jack struggled for words as he realized he was losing his audience. Finally, knowing he had to get their attention again, he "suddenly said something about prostitutes and pawnbrokers being 'Pardoned in Heaven, the first by the throne.'" The audience took notice. Gilmore described the rest of their time as "steel on steel and the laughter of good fellows, and answers that belonged to life."[17]

Gilmore was impressed by the way Jack restrained all emotion in his speaking, yet "his listeners knew instinctively that his thoughts had been hammered out in the furnace rather than stored inside a glacier." While some listeners entered the room feeling as if they were churning in the "confusion of a whirlpool," Jack showed them with "grace and clarity . . . a sterling and direct purpose." Repeatedly during the lectures, as they continued on throughout the year, Gilmore "saw the same result, sharp and clear as a diamond with many lights, whether he was speaking to a hundred or to a dozen."[18]

❋ ❋ ❋

The RAF lectures, which took Jack from The Kilns for two or three days at a time, caused a variety of problems. The travel by train was physically demanding, particularly when the trains were crowded, leaving him aching all over. If he traveled by night, the blackout restrictions meant he sat in a dark coach, unable to read and often cold. Traveling by day, he found consolation in seeing parts of the country he wouldn't otherwise have seen.

Trains in Wartime

On September 1, 1939, the British government took over the London Passenger Transport Board and the four railway companies that served the main lines of the country. The deal allowed each party a minimum annual income, with any amount over that to be equally divided. It proved to be a profitable enterprise for the companies.

For ordinary civilians, however, it was the start of the worst railway service they had experienced in their lifetimes. But getting upset or annoyed wasn't an option, since stations were plastered with posters suggesting that the travelers' sacrifice of convenience was vital to the war effort.

The posters didn't lie. During the war some 350,000 special trains were run for the military—each one using engines or coaches or trucks that would have been used for regular travel. Supplies, food, oil, and timber all had to be moved by train. All of the rubble created by the Blitz was removed from the cities by train and taken to other parts of the country to be used to build runways and bases. One historian reported, "By 1944 passenger trains were covering a third less mileage than before the war, but every one that did still run was squeezing in more than twice as many people."[19] Eventually, four hundred American army trains were brought in to help out, complete with American crews.

One hundred thousand men left the railways for military service, leaving stations and trains horribly undermanned. Much-needed maintenance work went undone. The rolling stock aged and became more and more dilapidated. Diminishing fuel reserves meant that trains ran slower. At the start of the war, any air-raid alert meant the train had to stop at the next station so passengers could find shelter—which could add hours to the journey.

To help thwart a German invasion, signs were removed from most of the larger stations, leaving passengers to guess where they were or alarmed to find they had missed their station or, often enough, discover they'd been on the wrong train for the entire journey.

The blackout took its toll as, at the beginning of the war, travelers had to ride in dark carriages. Passengers inadvertently sitting on each other became common enough—and so disagreeable that the government installed thin shafts of lights over seats. It wasn't until September 1944 that trains with curtains were allowed to use normal lighting for an entire journey.

For the average passenger, traveling at night was a creepy experience. Sitting in total darkness, one might hear whispers nearby but never see the faces of the speakers. A woman might doze, only to awaken with a sleeping man's head on her shoulder. Yet, surprisingly, personal assaults on dark trains were extremely rare.

With no light, it was impossible to read or do anything other than sit. For someone like Jack Lewis, this was an unbearable waste of good reading time.

As the trains became more crowded, finding a seat became nearly impossible. Some passengers stood for trips that lasted hours.

Hunger was a problem for travelers, as food service on the trains and in the stations either disappeared or became crowded to the point of inaccessibility. Station restaurants not only ran out of food but also plates, cups, and cutlery.

If a passenger was fortunate enough to bring something to eat, it might be a dried-egg sandwich or something made with spam or an apple. Passengers might share their food, upping the feast to boiled eggs, a tomato, or a piece of ham.

Soldiers were often welcome companions, if only for safety's sake, and sometimes led community singing. However, their packs—taking up room in the compartments or in the passageways—were easily tripped over. Or, in an airless carriage, weary soldiers might remove their boots for the night, much to the terror of the civilian passengers. A uniform often meant extra consideration would be given by the others. Space was made on packed trains for service men and women on leave, even if it meant civilians forfeited their seats or journeys to accommodate them. Often the station restaurants or remaining buffet cars would serve only the military.

Not everyone who served their country was given extra consideration, though. BBC presenter Freddy Grisewood stood for eight hours on a train from London to Sunderland, spoke to an audience of five thousand people, ate a bun and drank a cup of tea, then stood again for the eight-hour ride back to London.

Families taking the train for their holidays were warned they might be stranded. It was better to stay home. Posters asking, "Is your journey *really* necessary?" gave everyone second thoughts.

The totality of this travel experience was often at a premium cost, as discounted fares had disappeared for all but official workers getting to and from their jobs. Luggage limitations were introduced, even on personal items, and included—for a short time—a ban on flowers.

Yet for all the chaos and inconvenience, passengers were often kind and helpful, reaching out to give a hand to a woman with a baby or making room where no more room seemed possible. Total strangers often chatted like old friends about books, films, religion, happy holidays, or loved ones.[20]

✳ ✳ ✳

Late in April 1941, Eric Fenn met Jack in Oxford. They made plans for Jack's broadcast talks. But Fenn informed Jack that before anything else could be done, he needed a recording of Jack's voice. He had to make sure its tone and quality would work for a radio audience.

Jack agreed, and a recording was made in early May. Upon hearing his voice on playback, Jack was "unprepared for the total unfamiliarity of the voice; not a trace, not a hint, of anything one could identify with oneself—one couldn't possibly guess who it was."[21]

Welch and Fenn were suitably impressed with how Jack sounded. The next issue was about what he would *say*. As a starting point, Jack wrote and submitted an outline of the talks he would give. Jack stayed with his earlier view that the talks should explore the reality of a moral law before attempting any discussion about Christianity itself.

The title for the series hadn't been decided yet. Jack offered some descriptive suggestions, but Fenn thought they were dull. The two men went back and forth on alternatives for several weeks.

With Fenn's approval, Jack set to work on the actual scripts.

✳ ✳ ✳

There was a full moon over London on May 10, 1941, a perfect navigational tool for the German pilots who used it to guide them into the city and then back to France to refuel for another attack. This went on all through the night as over 570 sorties were flown. The German high command would claim that more than one hundred thousand incendiary bombs were dropped.[22]

The fire brigades across London were taxed to the limit as more than two thousand fires raged,[23] water mains broke, and supplies ran out. The Thames River had a low ebb tide that night, leaving the fire boats desolate. Swimming pools, canals, and ponds were sought out. Second and third waves of German bombs fell on the fire crews, killing many of them instantly.

When the all clear sounded the next morning, exhausted firefighters left many of the fires to burn out, leaving blocks of homes, hospitals, stores, and offices to the insatiable flames.

The night of bombing also damaged some of London's most famous landmarks, including the Tower of London, Westminster Abbey, many of London's museums and the houses of Parliament. More than fourteen hundred civilians—including the mayors of Westminster and Bermondsey—were killed, and over seventeen hundred were badly injured.[24]

No one in Britain knew then that May 10 would see the last major air attack on London until 1944. Hitler would turn his attention to the Soviet Union, redirecting his air force to areas farther east.

In a speech three days earlier that was almost prophetic, Winston Churchill said to the House of Commons, "When I look back on the perils which have been overcome, upon the great mountain waves through which the gallant ship has driven, when I remember all that has gone wrong, and remember also all that has gone right, I feel sure we have no need to fear the tempest. Let it roar, and let it rage. We shall come through."[25]

* * *

Jack sent two scripts to Fenn in early June 1941. Fenn's concern now wasn't about the content but getting the scripts to the correct length. The talks would be broadcast *live*, so each script had to be perfectly timed. Fenn knew that Jack's lack of experience behind the microphone meant he couldn't know the effect sheer adrenaline had on a broadcaster's energy, and even his sense of time and place. A listening audience must hear words at a pace that could be comprehended, but not so slow as to induce boredom.

Fenn also had to worry about gaps of silence—not because silence itself was bad but because the BBC feared any gaps of silence might be used by the Germans to break into the transmission. So the usual silences a speaker might include, if only to stretch time when a program was running short, had to be limited.

The scripts themselves had to be scrutinized by the BBC's censors to make certain that no unwanted or unintentional messages were included that might help the enemy or hurt the war effort.

How Jack was able to navigate this work in the midst of his other responsibilities was itself remarkable. When rejecting a different invitation from another BBC division, he stated that he was "talking already to the RAF, to the general public, to nuns, to undergraduates, to societies. The gramophone will wear out if I don't take care!"[26]

✳   ✳   ✳

On Sunday, June 8, 1941, Fred Paxford chauffeured Jack to the University Church of St. Mary the Virgin in Oxford. It was the largest church in the city and, historically, was the center point from which Oxford originally grew. Jack was there to preach the sermon for the Evensong service.

This was Jack's second sermon in the church. He had preached in October 1939, right after the war had begun, choosing the subject "None Other Gods: Culture in War-Time" (which was later published as the essay "Learning in War-Time").[27] His sermon then presented themes Jack would return to again and again: that war wasn't an aberration of normality but a heightened state of our true condition as we confront daily frustrations and even death (which every human experiences 100 percent of the time). He argued that education wasn't expendable in war but was vital to maintaining our humanity in the face of such horrors. The sermon caused enough of a positive reaction for the rector, T. R. Milford, to ask Jack to return.

Jack's growing reputation preceded him. The church was full long before the service began. As the last hymn, "Bright the Vision That Delighted," echoed out, Jack Lewis took to the podium. He titled his sermon "The Weight of Glory," based on the apostle Paul's second letter to the Corinthians: "For our light affliction, which is but for a moment, worketh for us a far more exceeding and eternal weight of glory."[28] He spoke for forty-five minutes. According to Erik Routley, a student sitting in the audience, Jack's words had a "stunning effect" for their combination of "sheer beauty and severe doctrine." Routley saw in Jack "a man who had been laid hold of by Christ and who enjoyed it."[29]

The sermon captured the totality of Jack's style and approach at this time in his life. He explored subjects such as unselfishness, love, following Christ, rewards, and heaven with a self-effacing ease, while taking to task any detractors of Christianity. Jack's poetic longing for beauty and eternity—*joy*, as he sometimes called it—served as the punctuation mark.

"At present we are on the outside of the world, the wrong side of the door," he said. "We discern the freshness and purity of morning, but they do not make us fresh and pure. We cannot mingle with the splendours we see. But all the leaves of the New

Testament are rustling with the rumour that it will not always be so. Some day, God willing, we shall get *in*."[30]

In the chronology of Jack's personal theology, "The Weight of Glory" fit perfectly after *The Problem of Pain* and *The Screwtape Letters* and as a lead-in to the first series of *Broadcast Talks* for the BBC.

C. S. Lewis, communicator to the masses, was ready to take the stage.

✳ ✳ ✳

Jack's original titles for the *Broadcast Talks*—*The Art of Being Shocked* or *The Humans*—were set aside. Together, Jack and Fenn decided on *Inside Information?* as the best title, with this description: "Four talks on the meaning of Right and Wrong."

The assistant director of program planning, Harman Grisewood, a cousin to BBC presenter Freddy Grisewood, shot off a memo to James Welch arguing against *Inside Information?* because leadership didn't care for it and found it "rather unseemly."[31] He argued that because it was wartime, "such a phrase might refer to sensitive information or even the fruits of espionage."[32]

Fenn conferred with Jack again, and by July 22, 1941, the two had settled on *Right and Wrong: A Clue to the Meaning of the Universe?*

Jack finished the initial drafts of the scripts in longhand, as he often did. It's unclear why Warnie wasn't able to type them up, but according to BBC journalist and author Justin Phillips, Jack's scripts arrived at the BBC to be typed there. A copy was sent for Jack to correct while Fenn sent copies around to the appropriate people within the BBC for review.[33]

Fenn remained anxious about the timing. Using a stopwatch,

he did his best to read the script as Jack might on the night of the broadcast. He assumed that as a novice, Jack might read more slowly than usual. He was alarmed to realize the first talk would be *under* by two or two and a half minutes. He asked Jack for adjustments to get the material closer to time. Even with those adjustments, Fenn established a backup plan: he would compensate for any lack of time with longer opening and closing announcements.[34]

DEFENDING THE FAITH

In spring of 1945, Jack Lewis was asked to speak to a conference of youth leaders and junior clergy at Carmarthen in Wales. The subject was Christian apologetics, which Jack quickly clarified as simply giving a defense of the faith. He gave advice to his audience, clearly gleaned from the experiences he'd had throughout the war.

He first asked his audience to consider what they might be defending—and to whom? To the first part of the question, he reminded his audience members to establish the true boundaries of their doctrines. To go beyond those boundaries would lead them so far away from the faith as to no longer be Christian. And if they were to do that, even if their intentions were sincere and honest, he hoped they would have the integrity to stop taking money from the church they now rejected and resign their positions.

Of more importance, Jack reminded his audience members that they were to defend *Christianity* and not their *opinions* of Christianity. They were to defend it because it is *true* and not because they liked it or believed it was good for people. And defending Christianity, as opposed to their own ideas, would force them to look at the faith fully, no matter how uncomfortable that might be.

Jack cautioned his audience to avoid reading fashionable but fleeting theological works espousing the latest doctrines—the modern kind that might be all the rage in theological circles but hadn't stood the test of a time-tested Christianity.

He encouraged his audience to "attack the enemy's line of communication. What we want," he argued, "is not more little books about Christianity, but more little books by Christians on other subjects—with their Christianity *latent*."[35] Reading a book about Christianity wouldn't affect people if they were already Christians or predisposed against Christianity. Reading a book on another subject, with an assumed Christianity within it, would impact people more effectively, even more so if the very *best* book on a given subject was written by a Christian. The twisting of any subject by a Christian in the name of evangelism would be the wrong thing to do.

The job of the apologist, Jack continued, is to present a timeless Christian message in the language of our own age, (as opposed to those who took the messages of the age and put them in the language of Christianity).

Be wary of preaching about politics, Jack instructed. Few have the right skills or knowledge to talk about politics credibly. More often than not, the only thing a sermon about politics does is tell the congregation which newspapers the preacher is reading.

He instructed his audience to give up thinking of their country as home and distant lands as mission fields. Home *is* the mission field now. To reach the people here and now, one must understand the language and thinking of the people.

Jack admitted that most of what he'd learned on this subject came from speaking to the RAF camps. From those servicemen, Jack learned that most were skeptical about history—including the Gospel accounts—only because it happened in the far past.

The present was far more real and believable. This skepticism also extended to old books, especially anything written before printing. Without the original manuscripts, the document was suspect.

Jack also found among the servicemen that there was no real understanding of sin. Sin, as traditionally understood, meant having a sense of guilt. The gospel, then, was truly good news because it would take care of that guilt and sin. Now, however, people had been trained to blame someone else for whatever was wrong. They judged God for having created such a messed-up world.

To that end, Jack warned his audience that it would do them no good trying to point to sins people didn't believe they'd committed or to things people didn't even regard as sins anymore.

Speaking the way lay people speak was critical to giving a defense of the faith. Jack exhorted them to stop using ancient words and phrases that simply weren't understood anymore. "Translate every bit of your Theology into the vernacular," he said. "I have come to the conviction that if you cannot translate your thoughts into uneducated language, then your thoughts were confused. Power to translate is the test of having really understood one's own meaning."[36]

If possible, Jack noted, use both intellectual and emotional means to speak to an audience. He said to be careful not to assume that uneducated people are, by default, irrational people. Go slowly enough, he explained, and the uneducated person will follow what's being said.

Avoid watering down Christianity by removing the supernatural, Jack said. Remove the supernatural, and there is little left in Christianity to make it attractive. Don't allow the arguments of science to distract you from the real arguments about the nature of humanity and God. And don't succumb to the modern notion that miracles were believed in ancient times because people didn't know any better. Miracles were understood in the same way we understand them now: as miracles. Joseph, for example, understood enough about how a woman could become pregnant naturally to recognize that "a virgin birth was contrary to Nature"[37] and therefore miraculous.

Avoid arguments about the existence of God, Jack cautioned. If one winds up arguing about the divinity of Christ, argue it from the absurdity and improbability that He could be called merely a good teacher. "The Lord's own words and claims . . . must be forced home," he said.[38]

Keep your audience's focus on the truth, Jack concluded. Christianity is *true*, not good. It isn't about good manners or morality or dispensed with because of corrupt priests or unfortunate events in history. Force your audience back to the "real point"—that Christianity, if true, is of "infinite importance" and, if false, "of *no* importance."[39] There is no middle ground.

Finally, Jack observed, the most dangerous thing to an apologist's faith is doing apologetic work. It's all too easy to neutralize one's faith—to make it unreal—by turning it into an object for debate. An apologist is most vulnerable directly after defending his faith in a debate. The arguments must be put away, and the reality of Christ, not the arguments, must be embraced anew.

And we must pray for one another.

It's unclear how Jack felt about these demands on his usual writing method. He was used to creating near-perfect first drafts when writing for any printed medium. Articles, essays, even novels were virtually pristine by the time he put down his pen after the last sentence. Accounting for time, receiving input from total strangers, and allowing for censorship changes had to seem intrusive.

Distance was also a problem. Jack was in Oxford. The Religious Broadcasting department had been relocated to Bedford. The series would be broadcast from London. Organizing all of the details from so many different points increased the time and energy it took to produce each script. Fenn might have been used to it as an experienced producer, but Jack certainly wasn't.

For the day of the first broadcast, Fenn made arrangements for Jack to meet him at the BBC's canteen at 6:30 p.m. The plan was to rehearse at 7:10 p.m. to make any last-minute adjustments. The broadcast itself was slated for 7:45, sandwiched between *News in Norwegian* and music from the National Eisteddfod of Wales. The Eisteddfod was a traditional Welsh festival of cultural songs and verse. In other words, an unknown Oxford tutor was going to speak on the subject of natural law to listeners who spoke Norwegian and cared about that country's news, or those interested in Welsh folk music.

This was an inauspicious beginning for three men who hoped to reach their culture for Christ.

"THE ART OF BEING SHOCKED"

Until the on-air light went on for Jack to begin his first broadcast on the evening of Wednesday, August 6, 1941, there was no way Fenn could predict what would happen. Was Lewis's script long? Short? Would he be engaging or slip into a dull monotone? It was anyone's guess. There is no record that Jack and Fenn met at the BBC canteen prior to the broadcast as Fenn had planned. Nor do we know whether they were able to rehearse or make any last-minute changes. On the contrary, Fenn indicated in his next letter to Jack after the first broadcast that "it would be wise to have a run-through of the script before the broadcast" to ensure timing and provisions for any gaps.[1]

"Good evening," Jack began:

Every one has heard people quarrelling. Sometimes it sounds funny and sometimes it sounds merely unpleasant; but however it sounds, I believe we can learn something very important from listening to the kind of things they say. They say things like this: "That's my seat, I was there first"—"Leave him alone, he isn't doing you any harm"—"Why should you shove in first?"—"Give me a bit of your orange, I gave you a bit of mine"—"How'd you like it if anyone did the same to you?"—"Come on, you promised." People say things like that every day, educated people as well as uneducated, and children as well as grown-ups.[2]

Jack began with a "hook"—something so normal in human behavior that it was bound to catch the listener's ear. "That's me," the listener might conclude and continue to listen.

Now what interests me about all these remarks is that the man who makes them isn't just saying that the other man's behaviour doesn't happen to please him. He is appealing to some kind of standard of behaviour which he expects the other man to know about.[3]

Jack took the most normal behavior and guided the listener to a deeper observation. He would then go even deeper as he explored the ways in which an unspoken or intuitive "Law" or "Rule" of fair play or good behavior is assumed by conflicting parties. These rules "used to be called the 'Law of Nature,'" he explained. And they are just as real as the law of "gravitation" or "laws of chemistry."[4]

the day ahead contained news reports, inspirational religious services, a program with advice about nutrition, a news-magazine show, news commentary for schools, and for this particular morning, the first of two broadcasts from the National Eisteddfod of Wales. More broadcasts for the schools, talks about first aid, and another music program took listeners to the noon hour and a variety show.

The afternoon included a fifteen-minute news update, another music program, a documentary examining how themes of love and war were handled by various composers, followed by *Music While You Work*—a mainstay of British broadcasting during the war and for years after, featuring morale-lifting and assembly-line-driving music. A garden show, fifteen minutes of recorder music, a rerun of the popular variety show *The Happidrome*, and then Welsh news and features filled out the time until the children came home from school.

The Children's Hour served as a lead-up to dinnertime, with a new radio dramatization of *Anne of Green Gables* by L. M. Montgomery. A few minutes were then given for daily prayers.

At six o'clock a more extensive news bulletin was presented, lasting half an hour, followed by an interview program. At seven, a show aired for the various Civil Defence forces, with morale-boosting talk, advice, and music. It also included a *Salute to Heroes* and entertaining interviews with everyday people.

If listeners were teetering on whether to keep their radios on or turn them off, *News in Norwegian*, broadcast in Norwegian, may have clinched their decisions. We can't know how many were listening when *Right and Wrong: A Clue to the Meaning of the Universe?* was announced, and C. S. Lewis began to talk about "Common Decency."

With every new point, Jack went back to a common experience, touching close to home, that if the "Law of Nature" wasn't right, then "all the things we say about the war are nonsense. What is the sense in saying the enemy are in the wrong unless Right is a real thing which the Germans at bottom know as well as we do and ought to practise?"[6]

Jack systematically raised his points, anticipated what the audience might reject, countered the rejection, and moved on to the next point, with practical and empathetic examples . . . and so on for the next dozen minutes. He concluded:

> Well, those are the two points I wanted to make tonight. First, that human beings, all over the earth, have this curious idea that they *ought* to behave in a certain way, and can't really get rid of it. Secondly, that they don't in fact behave in that way. They know the Law of Nature; they break it. These two facts are the foundation of all clear thinking about ourselves and the universe we live in.[7]

And then it was done.

After Lewis came a follow-up broadcast from the Welsh Eisteddfod festival, then *Under Suspicion*, a melodrama produced by Val Gielgud (actor John Gielgud's brother).

With no time for review or praise or criticism, both Jack and Fenn dashed off in separate directions to catch their trains— missing them would have been inconvenient. Jack certainly didn't want to get home late. Fenn informed Jack in his next letter that he not only caught his train but was also able to get a seat. Clearly neither man behaved as if he'd been part of something historic.

✳ ✳ ✳

Fenn was pleased with Jack's debut, all in all, but would worry about the timing of each talk throughout the series—and Jack would confound him to the very end by quickly adjusting the script, or his pacing, to get it right.

Both men now turned their attention to finalizing the script for the next talk. As letters from listeners arrived at the BBC, Fenn passed their questions on to Jack. Jack integrated the questions into the talks, giving him more leverage to make his points, eliminate confusion, and disarm potential arguments.

✳ ✳ ✳

On the next Wednesday, August 13, Jack returned to the studio for "Scientific Law and Moral Law." Picking up from where he left off in the previous talk, Jack contrasted the "Laws of Nature" with the "Laws of Human Nature," clarifying that the law of nature relates to what *will* happen versus the moral law of what *ought* to happen in human behavior.

With the usual drawn-from-life examples sprinkled throughout, he then concluded:

Consequently, this Rule of Right and Wrong, or Law of Human Nature, or whatever you call it, must somehow or other be a real thing—a thing that's really there, not made up by ourselves. And yet it's not a fact in the ordinary sense, in the same way as our actual behaviour is a fact. It begins to look as if we'll have to admit that there's more than one kind of reality; that, in this particular case, there is something above and beyond the ordinary facts of men's behaviour, and yet quite definitely real—a real law, which none of us made, but which we find pressing on us.[8]

Upon this argument, everything else would follow.

If there was any sense from Fenn that he recognized the genius behind Jack's talks, he hid it well. He candidly admitted to Jack that he considered this talk "turgid," if only because it was the most difficult.[9]

✳ ✳ ✳

Jack's third talk on August 20, 1941, dealt with "Materialism or Religion?" and found itself in a more agreeable place in the schedule—coming after Freddy Grisewood's program *The World Goes By* and before *The Marriage of Figaro* (directed by the esteemed conductor and composer Malcolm Sargent). Arguably, it brought Jack closer to what we might now call his "demographic."

On this occasion, Jack arrived with a cold and penciled in a note of explanation to his audience at the top of his script, with the proviso that if they suddenly heard a loud sound, not to assume that a bomb had gone off; he'd only sneezed or coughed.[10]

Even an informal comment suffered from editing. Likely at the insistence of Fenn, the reference to "being bombed" was cut for obvious reasons.[11]

Jack began with a summary of the previous talks, reminding his audience of the salient points that would lead them into consideration of a "materialistic" or scientific view, which can only experiment in order to *watch* how things behave in order to draw conclusions, versus the "religious view," which points to something behind all the evidence that science can only observe. It's the "why" behind the "how." This "Something"—a conscious mind—is at work and has preferences and purposes. It has put upon us the moral law.[12]

"Now, don't think I'm going faster than I really am," he said, anticipating his listeners' reactions. "I'm not yet within a hundred miles of the God of Christian theology. All I've got to is a Something which is directing the universe, and which appears in me as a law urging me to do right and making me feel responsible and uncomfortable when I do wrong."[13]

He wrapped up with a warning: "There's been a great deal of soft soap talked about God for the last hundred years. That's not what I'm offering. You can cut all that out."[14]

"MATERIALISM OR RELIGION?"

"Materialism or Religion?" contained examples of the kinds of changes and adjustments Jack had to consider for these broadcasts.

At one point Jack challenged the view that a huge power in a huge universe couldn't possibly be interested in humanity. To that view, his script described a man "who thinks a large building is necessarily better architecture than a small one is a blockhead and the man who thinks a large income makes its possessor a more valuable man is a snob. I don't think my legs [are] more important than my brain because they're bigger."[15]

Historian Justin Phillips noted that words like *blockhead* or even *snob* might have been considered inappropriate for the BBC's audience.[16] As it is, Lewis cut the entire section from the final published versions.

Lewis scholar Walter Hooper has pointed out the painstaking way in which Jack sought to find the right metaphor or analogy for his talks. In this talk, Jack had originally written, "If there was a controlling power outside the universe, it could not show itself to us as one of the facts inside the universe—no more than the author of a play could walk in as one of the characters *in* the play." One can imagine the ways in which he found that problematic, since an author *could* walk in as a character in a play. It was then adjusted in the script to "no more than the operator in a cinema could himself appear on the screen," which made more sense, though it didn't satisfy Jack. By the time he reworked the talks for the published version of *Broadcast Talks*, the example became "no more than the architect of a house could actually be a wall or staircase or fireplace in that house."[17]

After the broadcast, Fenn reported to Jack praise from Welch, who thought this talk was "excellent" and "the pace exactly right." Fenn, who clearly had his own reservations about the pacing of the talk, qualified that it was a case of "'when doctors disagree'—though my disagreement was small."[18]

❊ ❊ ❊

In the studio on August 27, 1941, Jack came to a key moment in the series. Titled "What Can We Do About It?," the talk began by anticipating an argument from some listeners that all his talk about a "Someone" or "Something" wasn't a matter of philosophy but of religion—and the world had moved on from religion, so he was merely trying to turn the clock back again.

Jack countered that going *back* to a truth wasn't counter to progress, if progress "means getting nearer to the place where you want to be." If you are on the wrong train, or the "wrong road," you have to go back to correct your journey.[19]

Jack then continued with his discussion about the Something, or Someone, and the evidence in the universe and in the moral law for its existence. The problem with getting to know that Someone through the universe is like trying to know the character of an architect through the design of a building. It may tell you a little, but not enough. A conversation will tell you a lot more, and the moral law is the start of that conversation. But what does it tell us? For one thing, it tells us that our understanding of what is "good" aligns with the "'good'" of the Someone behind the moral law, even if we fail to do that good. And this isn't a warm and fuzzy good but a "hard as nails"[20] good that is exacting and demanding. "Goodness is either the great safety or the great danger—according to the way you react to it," Jack stated.[21]

Jack pressed on with his argument: If that Someone isn't good, then all is lost for us. If that Someone *is* good, then we're at odds with the Someone because He is and we aren't. Jack then explained how Christianity begins to speak to people only after they realize there is a moral law they've broken, and a power behind that law that is now estranged from us. Realizing their terrifying position and the desperation of it, people may then find that Christianity offers the answer. It "tells people to repent and promises them forgiveness."[22]

It's not a source of comfort in the beginning but ultimately becomes one. "In religion, as in the war and in everything else, comfort is the one thing you can't get by looking for it," he said.

> If you're looking for truth, you may find comfort in the end: if you're looking for comfort you will not get *either* comfort *or* truth—only soft soap and wishful thinking to begin with and, in the end, despair. Most of us have got

over the prewar wishful thinking about international politics. It is time we did the same about religion.[23]

This "final" talk followed the popular show *Melody Unlimited,* raising the BBC's expectation of a large audience. Jack came to the conclusion he had intended all along for the series.

But it turned out not to be the final talk at all.

❋ ❋ ❋

The commission from Fenn was for four talks, but the volume of letters with questions led the BBC to ask Jack for a fifth talk to answer them. Jack agreed and sent Fenn his new script. Fenn, as usual, suggested cuts, especially one section where Jack had piled up illustrations.

Jack responded to Fenn with a handwritten note on a postcard. "I've done what I think will be sufficient cutting and we must do without the last para[graph]," he said.[24]

Coincidentally, the "Listeners' Questions" talk came on the second anniversary of the war. Falling as it did between *Can You Beat It?*, a comedy show, and *No Longer Alone*, a documentary about the war, Jack would have had millions of listeners that night.

In many ways, dealing with listeners' questions may have helped Jack with this "peak" audience. He was able to put forward answers that many of them puzzled over, even if they hadn't heard the first four talks. He argued against the moral law being merely "herd instinct" and discussed the benefits and follies of instincts themselves; he explored the objective realities of the moral law and the difference between the moral law and people's ideas of "Decent Behavior."

Fenn, in his "formal expression" of gratitude by letter to Jack, conceded, "the talks were really good," and that the fifth was "an excellent finish."[25]

✳ ✳ ✳

RAF officer John Lawler recalled standing in the officers' mess one night. Someone had just ordered a drink when Jack's voice sounded from the radio that had been playing in the background. Everyone froze where they were to listen. By the end of the talk, the barman realized he was still standing with his arm outstretched with the drink for the other man. They were so engaged they had forgotten what they were doing.[26]

✳ ✳ ✳

By any measure, the talks were a huge success.

The first indicator was the letters the BBC received. People of all backgrounds, with all kinds of needs, wrote to Jack for advice, consolation, information, or simply to express their appreciation. Some came from "lunatics who sign themselves 'Jehovah' or begin 'Dear Mr. Lewis, I was married at the age of 20 to a man I didn't love,'" Jack wrote. Many, however, came from "serious inquirers," and he felt it was his duty to give thorough answers.[27]

The effort, though, took more time and energy than Jack could manage. On one occasion he lamented to Fenn that he'd written thirty-five letters in one day.[28] Jack found letter writing fatiguing and costly, since he personally bore the cost of the postage. He hoped the BBC might step up to help somehow.

The second indicator of the series' success came with the immediacy of the BBC's request for a second series. The final talk was on September 3, 1941. On September 4, Fenn asked Jack to continue with *What Christians Believe* the following January and February.

Whatever frustrations or fatigue Jack felt at this time, he accepted the invitation only three days later.[29]

The Kilns, 1930

CHRISTIAN
BEHAVIOUR

C. S. LEWIS
Author of 'The Screwtape Letters'
and 'The Problem of Pain'

GEOFFREY BLES

ABOVE ▲

Seventh printing, 1948

C.S. Lewis, 1960

THE RIM OF THE WORLD

THE SUCCESS OF JACK'S TALKS for the Religious Broadcasting department led others in the BBC to offer him program opportunities. One included a new recording of the talks for Australia, which Jack declined because he didn't want to repeat his effort. He was asked to do other types of talks or appear on other existing broadcasts. Even Eric Fenn's request for him to do a series about worship was rejected. Jack wrote that he was simply too busy and declined them all.[1]

And busy he was. On Wednesdays in August 1941, listeners were hearing his voice on the radio. On every Friday from May to November, subscribers to the *Guardian* were reading installments of *The Screwtape Letters*. On the weekends RAF officers heard his lectures. Societies and committees had Jack's attention throughout the week. Students sat under him as their tutor. The Inklings met on Tuesdays and Thursdays.

In early October, Jack's publisher, Geoffrey Bles, asked to publish the talks he'd just finished for the BBC *and* the ones he hadn't begun to write. Jack also began work on the sequel to *Out of the Silent Planet* in which "the same man goes to Venus. The idea is that Venus is at the Adam-and-Eve stage: i.e. the first two rational creatures have just appeared and are still innocent. My hero arrives in time to prevent their 'falling' as *our* first pair did."[2] This book became *Voyage to Venus*, better known as *Perelandra*, which was published in 1943.

At The Kilns, Warnie had returned from his boat for the winter. He was able to help Jack with the growing number of letters. Mrs. Moore's bad health and domestic demands on Jack persisted.

In many ways, Jack's life continued at home as it had been, even as the momentum behind his speaking and writing increased.

* * *

Welch hadn't placed his hopes solely on Jack. The broadcast talk format was good, but he had pursued other ideas beyond it— one with a mutual friend: Dorothy Sayers. Jack had reviewed Sayers's book *The Mind of the Maker* for *Theology* magazine in October 1941.[3] He liked it, certainly more than he liked her detective fiction, which was a genre Jack didn't care for at all. They struck up a correspondence and friendship. She had invited him to write a book for a series she was editing, but he turned it down, convinced that she ought to write the book herself. Though she never actually attended an Inklings meeting, Jack considered her an unofficial member.

In 1938 Sayers had written a nativity play for the BBC called *He That Should Come*. It was a success. Now, in keeping with his newfound desire to put religious broadcasting on a level footing with entertainment, Welch asked Sayers to write a series of plays on the life of Jesus. She agreed, but with three conditions: "(1) She must introduce the character of Our Lord; (2) she must be allowed to use the same kind of realism which she had used in 'He That Should Come'; and (3) the plays must be in modern speech."[4]

Welch enthusiastically agreed, though they had to discuss just how far she could go with Jesus speaking in a modern style. Sayers was sensitive to the task, aware that there would be an outcry if she didn't get it right.

Val Gielgud was Sayers's choice for producer, having worked with him on the previous radio drama. He was unavailable. Instead, Derek McCulloch, an ongoing producer of *The Children's Hour*, was enlisted for the series.

During 1940 and 1941, Sayers worked on the scripts, finishing five of the twelve by Christmas 1941. The writing process had been fraught with conflicts, as an assistant director with *The Children's Hour* insisted on changes to Sayers's scripts. Sayers, an accomplished writer, took exception to the suggestions. A battle commenced, leading to Sayers canceling her contract with the BBC. Welch had to intervene, pulling the series from *The Children's Hour* entirely and bringing Val Gielgud in as producer.

Sayers was satisfied. She had a deep admiration for Gielgud and believed their mutual professionalism would create a great series.

Then, on December 15, 1941, Welch called a press conference to promote the first broadcast airing on Christmas Day. There, Sayers read a prepared statement on making the life of Christ vivid and believable. She offered a defense of her use of modern English and, using an actor to play Jesus, presented an example from the script.

She chose a fictional scene in which one disciple of Jesus—Matthew—teased another disciple—Philip—for allowing himself to be cheated in the marketplace. Matthew said, "Fact is, Philip my boy, you've been had for a sucker."[5]

The newspapers had a field day with such a loose interpretation. Headlines like "BBC 'Life of Christ' Play in U.S. Slang" adorned both the broadsheets and the tabloids.[6] The public reacted. Groups erupted in opposition. Churches held protests. Sayers personally received abusive letters and phone calls. Petitions were sent to both Prime Minister Churchill and William Temple, the archbishop of Canterbury. It came up in the House of Commons. Broadcasting House was called a "House of Blasphemy."[7] The actor hired to play Jesus—Robert Speaight—was accused of claiming to be God.[8]

DOROTHY SAYERS

Dorothy Sayers (1893–1957) was a novelist, essayist, poet, translator, and theologian. Born in Oxford, she was the daughter of an Anglican vicar who served as headmaster of the Christ Church Cathedral School in that city and, later, as parish minister in East Anglia. When she was eighteen, Sayers attended boarding school in Salisbury until she received a scholarship to Somerville College in Oxford. She returned to Oxford in 1912.

Upon completing her college education, she published two collections of poetry. In 1919 she traveled to the south of Normandy, in France, to teach English at a boarding school. Her fluency in French led to work translating French documents, and in 1920 she relocated to England to teach at a school near London.

Sayers was an avid reader and grew especially interested in mysteries. She used her time near London to read about criminology at the British Museum. As early as 1921 she explored ideas for detective stories and developed the character of Lord Peter Wimsey. Her first detective novel, *Whose Body?*, was published in 1923. Meanwhile she turned from teaching to advertising copywriting at a firm in London.

When she was about thirty years old, Sayers fell in love with a car salesman. She became pregnant, but the man refused to marry her. She kept her condition a secret from her elderly parents and gave birth to a son, John Anthony, in 1924 in a maternity home in Southbourne. Without financial support, she turned to her cousin Ivy Shrimpton for help to raise her son. Apart from Ivy, John Anthony, and the man Sayers later married, no one else knew of her secret. Subsequently Sayers met the former soldier and news reporter Oswald Arthur "Mac" Fleming. They married in 1926, and in 1935 they adopted Sayers's son.

Her career as a detective novelist gained momentum. Over the next decade she wrote more Lord Peter Wimsey books. She also made a name for herself writing dramas for various Church of England festivals, spearheaded by George Bell, the dean of Canterbury Cathedral and, later, the bishop of Chichester. She also began a guild for writers that aspired to stimulate creativity and "the Resurrection of the Faith, the Revival of Learning and the Re-integration of Society."[9]

In 1939, the BBC invited Sayers to write radio plays for them, at first as part of their *Children's Hour* program and, later, on their own. She also wrote about creativity in the 1941 book *The Mind of the Maker*. During this time she became friends with C. S. Lewis and Charles Williams. Through Williams, she took an interest in the thirteenth-century writer Dante Alighieri and soon embarked on a translation of *The Divine Comedy*. Part 1 was published in 1949 and part 2 in 1955.

Sayers died in 1957. She was buried in the tower of St. Anne's Church on Dean Street in London. Jack Lewis composed a glowing eulogy for the memorial service, held on January 15, 1958.

During the settling of Sayers's estate, John Anthony revealed his true identity as her son. Sayers's goddaughter, Barbara Reynolds, completed Sayers's translation of *The Divine Comedy* in 1962 and became her official biographer.[10]

Welch was resolute. He sent scripts to the Central Religious Advisory Committee, chaired by the bishop of Winchester and whose thirteen members represented the major denominations in the country. The committee unanimously backed Welch and Sayers's plays but insisted on reviewing every script so they could offer comments. Only through Welch's skillful diplomacy did Sayers agree.[11]

The plays finally aired between December 1941 and October 1942. The public reacted favorably. People from all walks of life commended Sayers and the BBC for giving them a fresh view of Jesus. The times for Evensong services were changed to allow listeners to hear the full program before coming to church. Non-churchgoers listened as well, finding themselves caught up in a story they thought they knew but didn't. Sayers received new letters of appreciation from grateful listeners.

Lewis heard only one of the plays but read the scripts. He reported to Arthur Greeves that they were "excellent, indeed most moving." He dismissed all the objections as "silly."[12]

✳   ✳   ✳

By mid-November 1941, Jack was hard at work on *What Christians Believe*, the five new talks for the BBC, slated to air on Sunday afternoons in January and February of 1942. Because he was tackling more weighty theological matters and wanted to avoid any accusations of denominationalism, he sought input from theologians in the Anglican, Roman Catholic, Methodist, and Presbyterian churches. The Presbyterian was Eric Fenn himself.

The scripts were finished by late November. Fenn was effusive in his praise of Lewis, calling the scripts "first class. . . . [T]here is a clarity and inexorableness about them, which made me positively gasp!" But timing, as before, was an issue. Fenn again thought they were on "the short side."[13]

* * *

In December 1941, Jack took on yet another job.

Stella Aldwinckle of St. Aldates Church in Oxford established a club for undergraduates to discuss and debate questions about the Christian faith. Her plan was to present a forum where the views of atheists and agnostics, or those disenfranchised from the church, could have their questions answered by the leading Christian thinkers of the day. It was named the Socratic Club. Jack became its president and used his considerable network of colleagues, Inklings, even acquaintances by mail, to enlist presenters. The Socratic Club's first meeting was on January 26, 1942, at Somerville College in Oxford. Jack's longtime friend and doctor Robert "Humphrey" Havard addressed the question, "Won't Mankind Outgrow Christianity in the Face of the Advance of Science and Modern Ideologies?"[14]

* * *

The war in Europe had been a different sort of conflict for the United States. President Franklin D. Roosevelt had wanted to publicly side with Winston Churchill and Great Britain against Hitler and the German army, but there was a formidable isolationist movement that insisted the United States stay neutral. Roosevelt did all he could, using every legal loophole available, to help the British, but he was frustrated. And Churchill was desperate as Britain's financial and military resources dwindled away in a war of attrition.

By September 1941, Roosevelt went so far as to say privately to Churchill that the US navy would become more and more provocative in the Atlantic Ocean to force an incident that would justify his bringing the United States into the conflict.[15]

On September 4, 1941, a U-boat attacked the US destroyer *Greer*. Roosevelt used the incident as an excuse to launch an unofficial, undeclared naval war against Germany. American warships would now escort British and Canadian convoys carrying much-needed food, fuel, and supplies. In November, the Neutrality Act of 1935, which had bound Roosevelt's hands for so long, was repealed by Congress. The president immediately armed American merchant ships and sent them to Britain.

Yet the antiwar feeling in America remained strong. It would take more than a U-boat attack to stir up the people's passions. Few expected the inciting act to come from a small Pacific island.

✳ ✳ ✳

In the 1930s Japan systematically invaded countries throughout Indochina, with very little response from the West, apart from protests and embargoes. The military might of Russia had been the most effective deterrent against the Japanese—along with the main fleet of American ships at Pearl Harbor, Hawaii.

In June 1941, Germany attacked Russia. The Japanese, released from any fear of Russian reprisal, overran what was left of Indochina, taking control of French possessions there. Those who were watching expected Japan to turn its eyes on the southeast, attacking areas owned by the British and Dutch.

The surprise to everyone, including the experts, came on the morning of December 7. Japanese planes bombed the American fleet in Pearl Harbor, sinking or damaging seven battleships and killing more than twenty-four hundred civilians and military personnel.[16]

OVER THERE: AMERICA INVADES BRITAIN

With the United States' entrance into the war, American soldiers were quickly enlisted and deployed to Europe. Great Britain was the first stop for many. The leadership at the US War Department realized that many Americans had never been overseas before and feared unnecessary conflict, out of ignorance, would strain relations between the two countries. To mitigate the problem, the war department created a pamphlet to help the young GIs get along with their British cousins. Titled *Over There: Instructions for American Servicemen in Britain, 1942*, the pamphlet gave very direct instructions. For example: [17]

- Americans, in general, needed to put aside any feelings they might harbor against the British because of the American Revolution or War of 1812. Irish Americans needed to forget their issues with the English as oppressors of the Irish. They were encouraged to think more about what the two nations had in common.

- The British were reserved in their sensibilities, but that shouldn't be confused with unfriendliness. They might not initiate conversation in trains or buses. When American GIs got to know them, they would find them open and honest.

- Different accents, money, customs, and phrases didn't make one culture superior to another; it was simply different. GIs should respect the differences without arguing about them.

- Many British words and phrases were different from American ones. *Bloody* was often used but offensive. A *bum* wasn't a bedraggled homeless person but a person's backside. The British called automobile fuel *petrol* instead of *gas*. A wrench was called a *spanner*. A small truck was called a *lorry*.

- The British system of money was unlike the American system and structured differently. It was inappropriate to talk about wages, since, in general, Americans made more than the British.
- Servicemen were told, "The British don't know how to make a good cup of coffee. You don't know how to make a good cup of tea. It's an even swap."[18]
- Instructions included these warnings: Don't show off or brag. Don't be unnecessarily loud or brash. Don't make fun of accents. Don't comment on British politics, and never criticize the king or queen. Don't make jokes about past wars, the defeats in this war, or war debt. Don't criticize or make jokes about the food, beer, cigarettes, or meagerness of the meals (since the British had been at war since 1939 and were under strict rations).
- The British were described as a "kindly, quiet, hard-working people who have been living under a strain such as few people in the world have ever known. In your dealings with them, let this be your slogan: 'It is always impolite to criticize your hosts; it is militarily stupid to criticize your allies.'"[19]

The British gave the pamphlet a lot of attention, since it allowed them to see how they were perceived by outsiders. The *London Times* (July 14, 1942) suggested the pamphlet should be a best seller and owned by all British readers. Later, the Strand Film Company would create the movie *A Welcome to Britain* to help the arriving servicemen. It touched on subjects the war department pamphlet didn't address, such as those from the American South needing to cope with blacks and whites sharing train compartments, pubs, or movie theaters, or dancing interracially at nightclubs.

On December 8 the United States declared war against Japan, and President Roosevelt sent a cable to Winston Churchill: "Today all of us are in the same boat with you and the Empire, and it is a ship which will not and can not be sunk."[20]

It was a foregone conclusion that war with Germany would happen next. It did on December 11, when Japan's ally Adolf Hitler declared war on America. Within a few hours, America responded with its own declaration.

Since 1939, Britain had come close to the brink of financial ruin and physical annihilation. Churchill and the British people had stood alone against the Nazi onslaught since the fall of France in June of 1940. Now the United States, with all of its vast resources, had joined the fight.

That night Churchill went to bed and "slept the sleep of the saved and thankful."[21]

✳ ✳ ✳

Curiously, the five BBC talks in Jack's second series weren't given titles as they had been for the first series. They were later named as chapters in the published version of *Mere Christianity*.

Jack began the first talk on January 11, 1942,[22] by looking at alternative religions. Each belief system contains some hint of the truth, he explained, but doesn't capture the truth as fully as Christianity. He also touched on different belief systems—along with atheism, which he argued was "too simple." He explained, "If the whole universe has no meaning, we should never have found out that it has no meaning."[23]

The second talk[24] took on the notion that one could believe in a "good God in Heaven" and leave out all the "terrible doctrines about sin and hell and the devil, and the redemption."[25] Jack also dealt with Christianity versus dualism, which positioned the concepts of good and evil as equal and independent powers.

On February 1, Jack explored the issue of free will,[26] explaining why the absence of free will would make human beings "hardly . . . worth creating." Being united with God must happen as a result of freedom and choice and not as an "automata" directive.[27] Here Jack spelled out how the history of free will led to the delusion that humans could become gods and find happiness in themselves, apart from the God who had created them. This delusion, Jack argued, has led to all of humanity's problems and an estrangement from our Creator.

Suddenly, a man showed up—the one called Jesus—and shocked everyone by claiming to be God and able to forgive sins and mend the estrangement between humanity and God.

Jack concluded by challenging the popular idea that Jesus could be accepted as a "great moral teacher,"[28] but not as God. He argued that Jesus didn't leave that as an option. To do what Jesus did and say what He said made Him a liar, a lunatic, or . . . who He claimed to be: God incarnate.

Welch considered this the "best of the series so far and quite admirable both in content and manner."[29]

The fourth talk, broadcast February 8, 1942,[30] dealt with atonement, which proved to be difficult for Jack, since *how* atonement worked varied so much from denomination to denomination. That it *did* work in the death of Christ was the main point he wanted to make. With handwritten adjustments to his original broadcast script, he wrote, "A man can accept what Christ has done without knowing how it works: indeed he won't begin to have any chances of knowing how it works *until* he's accepted it."[31]

In the final broadcast[32] Jack pursued the ways in which God spreads a "new kind of life"[33] through baptism, belief, and the Lord's Supper. After touching on these three necessities, Jack explained the authority of Christ behind them, the love of God *making* us good rather than God loving us *because* we're good, the need for these practices even if we consider them crude or unspiritual, the question of being saved through Christ alone, and God's desire for us to join Him freely before He truly invades our lives.

In the middle of the five talks, the BBC tried to draw Jack into a popular, but controversial, program called *The Brains Trust*, in which popular intellectuals took on questions of the day. Jack initially turned down the invitation but later joined in for one show in the spring. The experience was not a good one for him; he was trounced by evolutionary biologist and eugenicist Julian Huxley.[34] Jack wasn't alone, however, as other discussions about religion on the program often turned vitriolic. The BBC, sensitive about maligning faith and the role of the clergy in a time of war, eventually opted to keep religious subjects away from the program. Later, Welch had a hand in creating an alternative round-table religious discussion program called *The Anvil.*

Just before Jack finished the second broadcast series, his next work hit the bookstores and secured his place as a formidable and best-selling author.

❋ ❋ ❋

The Screwtape Letters was published in England on February 9, 1942.[35]

If anything could move Jack into the public's awareness, this book was it. Critics loved it; readers bought it. The book had to be reprinted eight times in its first year of release.[36] Suddenly this tutor and fellow of Magdalen College, the essayist and sometime broadcaster, was nationally known.

✳ ✳ ✳

In his unqualified praise for the second series of broadcast talks, Fenn quickly asked Jack to do yet another series in the autumn, this time for the Forces Programme (which was also heard by civilians) with subjects relevant to the soldiers. Since Jack was still lecturing to the RAF, it was an easy fit.

Jack agreed but used the opportunity to again appeal for help with the many letters he'd been receiving. Not only did mail come to him directly, but the BBC also forwarded the letters it received. Jack suggested the BBC use its magazine *The Listener* as a place to publish the scripts of the talks so readers could respond there. The BBC refused, citing space limitations.

Though he was frustrated by the BBC's lack of help, Jack agreed to do another series. He provided a sketchy outline in June 1942 that covered "Ordinary Ethics—Fair Play," "How Christianity Makes a Difference," "Christianity and Pleasure," "Chastity," "Humility," "Charity," "Hope and Faith as Virtues," and "The Problem of Faith and Works."[37]

Fenn asked Jack to name the forthcoming series. On August 15, Jack put forward *Christian Ethics*[38] as the working title but wasn't sure how that would translate in the vernacular. "Christian Morals? Christian Morality? Christian Moral Standards? Christian Behaviour?" He liked "Christian Behaviour" best, stating, "If Aristotle were writing now he'd call the Ethics 'Behaviour.'"[39] Jack also wondered if *The Christian Technique of Living* might be preferable.

Welch approved *Christian Behaviour* as the name for the series. But the month leading up to the broadcasts was fraught with problems.

✳ ✳ ✳

Before the launch of the next series of *Broadcast Talks* on September 20, 1942, Jack let Fenn know he would be speaking to the RAF in Cornwall. He provided an address, just in case any last-minute details needed handling.

They did.

On September 15, Fenn wrote to Jack that the scripts had been written for *fifteen*-minute broadcasts—the established time for the previous two series. Unfortunately, the sessions in the third series were slotted for *ten* minutes. Jack had to cut roughly one-third of the material in a matter of days.

But there was more to Fenn's letter. The fourth talk in the series—about sex and marriage—had been scrutinized very closely. Talk about sex on the public airways wasn't commonly accepted, nor was there a unified view about the subject among all of the Christian denominations. Fenn, being an astute producer, suggested changes to Jack's material to keep the audience from becoming distracted from his main points. It was a testimony to Fenn's diplomacy and Jack's patience that Jack agreed to all of Fenn's changes.

Even so, the broadcast about sex and marriage still caused controversy. Under the headline "This Was a Very Frank Talk Which We Think Everyone Should Read,"[40] the *Daily Mirror* sensationalized the talk by publishing the entire script without permission.

"Damn their impudence" was Jack's reply after Fenn informed him.[41]

✳ ✳ ✳

In the midst of this, Geoffrey Bles/Centenary Press published *Broadcast Talks: Right and Wrong: A Clue to the Meaning of the Universe?* and *What Christians Believe*. Jack had gone through the scripts and revised them for publication.

To the casual observer, the sudden appearance of books and broadcasts from C. S. Lewis must have been startling. He was an overnight sensation, more than forty years in the making.

✳ ✳ ✳

In the third series, Jack approached his subjects with the same candor, lucidity, and practicality as he had during the previous talks. Using the overarching example of ships in a convoy, he presented three purposes of morality in the first talk:[42] harmony *between* individuals, harmony *within* individuals, and clarification of the purpose of human life. Next he tackled the seven virtues, dealing first with the four known cardinal* virtues of prudence, temperance, justice, and fortitude.[43]

Having laid that foundation, Jack then took on "Social Morality"[44] in the second talk, explaining that it wasn't a political system or social system to be run by others, but a means by which we learn to love our neighbors after learning to love and obey God.

The third talk, broadcast October 4, 1942, went into specifics of "Morality and Psychoanalysis," differentiating the medical theories behind psychoanalysis itself and the general philosophical views of Freud, Jung, and others of that ilk. Further, Jack examined the two aspects of moral choice: the first being the

---

* Latin for "hinge of a door" or "pivotal."

act of choosing, and the second being the "raw material" of feelings and impulses that go into that choice. The raw material is, in some ways, diseased, which then affects the act of choosing. The raw material may even be "cured" by some means, but the choice is still made freely, even if it's a "bad" choice—and that is what morality is concerned with. Jack then stated that humans judge one another by actions, since that's all humans can see, whereas God judges moral choices. There is no bargaining with God about this. He knows that our freely made choices define us, turning us into creatures suitable for heaven or for hell.[45] "When a man is getting better he understands more and more clearly the evil that is still left in him," Jack said. "When a man is getting worse, he understands his own badness less and less."[46]

With "Sexual Morality" and "Christian Marriage," the two subjects of the fourth talk,[47] Jack clarified misconceptions about the Christian view of sex, the unpopularity of "chastity," and confusion about our natural appetites and how they've been distorted through propaganda: "They'll tell you sex has become a mess because it was hushed up. But for the last twenty years it has *not* been hushed up. It has been chattered about all day long. Yet it is still in a mess." He asserted that "the human race originally hushed it up because it had become such a mess."[48] Having dealt with what is *wrong* with the sexual impulse, he then put forward the correct Christian view of sex within marriage and what it means for a man and woman to become "one flesh." Here he tore apart modern views of romance and "falling in love" versus the Christian view of love as sacrifice. In his usual unflinching manner, he dealt directly with divorce and the "headship" of the husband over the wife.[49]

"Forgiveness," the next talk,[50] began with a correction. Jack had suggested that chastity was the most unpopular of virtues. He was now inclined to believe that the most unpopular virtue was forgiveness. "Every one says forgiveness is a lovely idea, until they have something to forgive, as we have in war-time,"[51] he stated. How can one forgive? What did Jesus mean by loving your enemy? Can one really hate the sin but love the sinner? Can one forgive the Nazis? In the end, Jack said, forgiveness is really about loving unlovable people—people like us, in fact.

THE CHURCH IN WARTIME

Not surprisingly, the outbreak of the war in 1939 triggered an increase in overall church attendance throughout Great Britain. By 1942, congregations seemed to decline. Many people relegated the church to the position of a spiritual emergency room where they would go if they were in crisis.[52]

There were many reasons for a decline in church attendance, apart from a lack of faith or interest. Fuel rationing kept more people at home. The nightly blackouts made travel difficult, if not deadly, on foot, on bike, or by car—and impacted basic lighting for evening services.

And the ease with which church members could listen to worship services on the BBC often aided a churchgoer's decision not to attend. Major events—like the fall of France—also kept people at home so they could hear the latest news.

Often, attendance in a church would *increase* after the church had been damaged or destroyed by German bombs. Author Norman Longmate recalled how his church was totally destroyed and "the congregation joined in the hymns and prayers . . . in the nearby infants school far more heartily than in the old building. When the elderly priest celebrated mass in a classroom decorated with children's drawings and multiplication tables, he seemed spiritually, as well as physically, far closer to his flock than he had ever done in the vast Victorian chancel of his church."[53] For some, it was as if they didn't appreciate how much church had meant to them until it was bombed.

A bombed-out church also pushed parishioners—and clergy—across denominational lines, as a congregation might be allowed to join another following a loss of worship space. Some members would never return to their original denomination. Even without overt destruction, old rivalries and suspicions were set aside. Clergy from the various churches often united for prayer services and special religious events.

The clergy were exempt from military service, though many still enlisted and served. Those who remained were often overwhelmed with additional duties, even serving multiple congregations on the same Sunday in different towns. The clergy frequently served with ARP and were often out all night helping the injured and survivors in bombed-out areas.

Churches served their parishes faithfully by praying for those who had gone off to war and by making public the names of those who had fallen. Parish bulletins and magazines, often ignored or mocked in peacetime, became important reminders of home to the servicemen who received them. Many of the church buildings were used as shelters—and the result often impacted the parish more than any bombs. Vestries, classrooms, meeting halls, and sections of the sanctuary were converted into first aid centers, canteens, and even barracks. Church coffee times and breakfasts went on, though rationing meant that parishioners often brought supplies, such as much-needed sugar or butter.

The rationing of clerical clothing caused a great debate as the

Board of Trade placed a higher coupon value on a priest's clothes than that of other workers but didn't give the priests additional coupons to purchase them. Complaints followed, as clergy felt cheated that a "bricklayer could get extra coupons for his overalls but a priest could not for his . . . cassock."[54] The Board of Trade argued that the clergy could wear their cassocks in place of a suit, while other workers couldn't do the same with their overalls or uniforms.

Some clergy rebelled against other government restrictions. One vicar persisted in ringing his church bells in spite of regulations forbidding it. A policeman persuaded him otherwise. Another vicar wasn't allowed to make a telephone call because the operator determined the call wasn't essential or official. The vicar informed her that his call was being made on behalf of the Almighty. The operator replied that the name of the Almighty wasn't on the priority list.

It was a natural follow–up to move from forgiveness to "The Great Sin"[55] of pride, "which has been the chief cause of misery in every nation and every family since the world began."[56] With the kinds of insights he showed in *The Screwtape Letters*, Jack listed the many manifestations of pride, including superiority, greed, and, worst of all, the inability to know God. "As long as you are proud you can't know God at all," since proud people are always looking down on things and, if looking down, they can't see what's above them.[57] Jack also examined humility and how easily it gets twisted up by the Devil, our pride, or our own misunderstanding of what humility actually is. From there he touched on the theological virtues of "Charity," contrasting Christian love against "natural likings" and affection, and then

"Hope," contrasting various views with the Christian view, which is hope firmly rooted in reality.[58]

In the final two talks,[59] Jack set his sights on "Faith," taking time to explain the two different senses of the word. The first sense means "simply Belief—accepting or regarding as true the doctrines of Christianity,"[60] with the use of human reasoning, regardless of emotions, with a recognition of our spiritual bankruptcy, and—surprise—with the understanding that faith actually comes from God Himself. Faith, in the second and "higher" sense, takes this reality further and puts everything we are or hope to be in God's hands, knowing that we can't muster faith even while we try. With remarkable dexterity, Jack placed faith and works together, positioning the question about which is more important akin to "asking which blade in a pair of scissors is most necessary."[61] He invoked the puzzling but not surprising admonishment from the Bible to "work out your own salvation with fear and trembling: For it is God which worketh in you."[62] Both faith and works are contained in that one passage.

In case the audience was mistaking Jack's broadcasts for pep talks on good behavior, he ended them with a qualifier: The "duties and rules and guilt and virtue" are meant to be the starting point. They're meant to take us into "something beyond." And using language that echoed the voice of Screwtape and foreshadowed Narnia, he pointed to the "glimpse of [another] country." In that country talk of such things isn't necessary, except "as a joke"—a place where everyone is "filled full" with goodness "as a mirror is filled with light"; where they don't think about goodness because they're "too busy looking at the source" of the light; a place where "the road passes over the rim of our world. No one's eyes can see very far beyond that: though lots of people's eyes can see further than mine."[63]

✼ ✼ ✼

There was a natural continuity to the series that listeners appreciated, following smoothly from the previous two series with a particular ease, as if no time had passed since they were broadcast. Jack had become a familiar and welcome voice. A series from C. S. Lewis every six months would have been an acceptable routine for the audience's listening habits, perhaps indefinitely.

They couldn't know it would be eighteen months before they'd hear him in a series again.

THE HIGH COST OF SUCCESS

JACK'S STAR WAS ON THE ascendancy in the public realm and certainly among Christians in Britain and now even America. At Oxford, however, Jack had "transgressed an unwritten code" by "behaving in a way that was intolerable and incorrect by the standards of Oxford society,"[1] according to George Sayer, who studied at Oxford under Jack.

Much as using the wrong knife or fork at the table might be frowned upon, so would engaging in a conversation beyond one's position. "A man who taught English or French literature might discuss academic questions with another specialist in the same subject, but it would be wrong for him to give his opinions on the classics or theology."[2]

J. R. R. Tolkien commented that Oxford dons could be forgiven for just about anything, except writing outside their subjects or "writing popular works of theology."[3]

With the publication of *The Pilgrim's Regress* in 1933, Jack was resented for crossing the line into an area where he had no business. "It was commonly thought that a man's belief is a private affair, and should not be written about or published."[4]

That he wrote satirically against philosophy and church divisions didn't help.

In the surge of creative activity begun in 1940, Jack broke all the unspoken rules at Oxford. *The Problem of Pain* was bad enough for some, but *The Screwtape Letters* was even worse for others. Also, to broadcast talks on the BBC that not only advocated Christianity but also sought to convert the listener was academically blasphemous. He was accused of having a religious mania. His colleagues believed he should limit himself to writing scholastically and looked with undisguised disdain on his populist works.

As early as 1944, *Time* sent a reporter to do an interview with Jack for the magazine.[5] The article wouldn't appear until 1947, but it would feature him on the cover and marvel over his insights and wit, even calling him a "heretic" among academics for daring to believe in God. The reporter had it right.

As late as 1951, Jack was outvoted for Oxford's prestigious poetry chair by 194 votes to 173. Irish poet Cecil Day-Lewis won. In his diary on February 8, 1951, Warnie wrote how surprised he was by the "virulence of [anti-Christian] feeling" toward Jack. Good friend Hugo Dyson informed Warnie how "one elector whom he canvassed announced his intention of voting for [Cecil Day-Lewis] *on the ground that* [Jack] had written *Screwtape!*"[6]

Jack's closest friends warned him that his religious endeavors would wreck his academic career. To that he responded as General William Booth of the Salvation Army had once responded to author Rudyard Kipling, "Young man, if I could win one soul for God—by playing the tambourine with my toes, I'd do it."[7] According to one colleague, that was precisely the thing they thought he was doing.

✳ ✳ ✳

Fortunately, a different view of Jack was held outside Oxford.

In February 1943, Jack and Warnie drove north to Durham for Jack to deliver three talks as part of the prestigious Riddell Memorial lectures. Founded in 1928 in memory of British barrister Sir John Walter Buchanan-Riddell, the lectures were created to address the relationship between religion and the contemporary development of thought. Jack's lectures were delivered in Newcastle on the evenings of February 24, 25, and 26, and were later published as *The Abolition of Man*.

In the lectures Jack continued themes he'd been exploring in the BBC lectures: the moral law (or "Tao," as he called it there) and the follies of subjectivism. The third lecture gave Jack a chance to play the Ghost of Christmas Yet to Come as he considered what a world ruled by subjectivism would look like.

The three days at the university and Durham Cathedral were restorative for Jack and Warnie, giving Jack a much-needed break from his duties at the college and The Kilns.

✳ ✳ ✳

Christian Behaviour and the novel *Perelandra* were released within a day of each other (April 19 and 20, 1943). *Perelandra*— or *Voyage to Venus*—was the second installment of what would become a trilogy of science fiction novels.

It was five months after the third broadcast series before Eric Fenn approached Jack about a fourth. On March 10, Fenn suggested a series examining "Misconceptions of Christianity."[8] He hoped to broadcast them in July and August but was willing to entertain other options.

Jack agreed to do a series, but not in those months. He

suggested later in the year.[9] Fenn countered in April with an invitation for Jack to do a single talk as part of another series titled *Why I Believe In God*, giving a more personal account of his faith. Again Jack declined, explaining that his history was so "mixed up" with philosophy as to be "useless" to the general public. And "personal testifying," while important, wasn't his gift.[10]

Welch had even more ideas. He asked Jack to appear on the new program called *The Anvil*—it was *The Brains Trust* discussion format redone for religious topics. Welch added, as an enticement, that the program wasn't live but was recorded over a three-hour period on Mondays.

The convenience of an evening time *and* recording without the pressure of a live performance *plus* a discussion rather than writing a script led Jack to say yes, providing the Monday didn't fall during the academic term. It took a lot of corresponding back and forth between the two men, but a date was finalized for July.

Fenn, seeing a new opportunity, wrote again to Jack, this time asking him to give a talk about *Paradise Lost* on the Home Service. Presumably Fenn chose this topic because of Jack's published *A Preface to Paradise Lost*.

Jack apologized again for refusing but suggested the talk would be a "waste of time." He wrote, "What's the good of telling them they'll enjoy it, when we both know they won't?"[11]

Having failed with alternatives, Fenn returned with a renewed invitation to take on another series of talks—as they'd discussed before. Fenn drolly suggested that rather than deplete Jack's supply of scrap paper, they should meet up to talk about it.

In mid-June, Jack submitted to Fenn a list of possible topics for the next series of talks. They included the doctrine of the Trinity, creation, the incarnation, the "Two Natures," the resurrection, and the ascension.[12]

Later, in a wry letter to Fenn confirming the date for his appearance on *The Anvil*, Jack used an *entire* sheet of paper with ample space around the letter itself, which Jack invited Fenn to use however he wanted.

Jack, Welch, and Fenn were reunited in London on July 19 for the recording of *The Anvil* program. The next letter from Fenn expressed how good it had been to see Jack again and how well the recordings seemed to be going.[13]

Fenn also confirmed the topics for the next series and the dates they would broadcast from January through March of 1944. He expressed his wish to have the scripts by November and assumed they wouldn't "quarrel violently" over them.[14]

✳ ✳ ✳

The first hint of trouble came in early August when the BBC bumped Jack's series in the schedule in favor of another on *Science and Religion*. This took Jack out of the January slot and pushed him to February and March.

Presumably Jack assumed the bump in the schedule gave him more time to work on the scripts. But on December 8, Fenn wrote to inquire about their progress. Jack indicated he'd written the scripts but couldn't find a typist to copy them. Understandably, he didn't want to send his originals in the mail. Fenn offered an alternative—Jack would give them to an Oxford barrister, who was also appearing on the BBC, for hand delivery.[15]

✳ ✳ ✳

Mrs. Moore had developed varicose ulcers, an extremely painful condition involving sores on her legs. She couldn't work and relied on Jack and evacuee June Flewett, who'd become a member of the household, all the more. Additionally, Fred Paxford had been taken away by the war effort to work in a car factory in Cowley. Muriel, "a kind of lady gardener and 'help'" proved to be depressed and often hysterical, "going into rages, and losing her faith." She needed an operation but continually put it off. Then there was "poor dear Margaret," a "certified 'mental deficient' maid" who was often humble and affectionate, but "subject to fits of inexplicable anger and misery."[16] For Jack, there never seemed to be a time when all of the women in the house were doing well.

By October 1943, Muriel's condition had declined to the point of hospitalization, with the doctor wanting to bring in a psychoanalyst to put her in a mental hospital. Mrs. Moore came to the rescue by having a "little quiet talk and *truth* (which the patient never [seemed] to get from doctors)"[17] and snapped Muriel back to her right mind. She took treatment in an ordinary hospital.

In spite of the drama, Jack felt "Christ in the house as I have never done before—but alas, such a house for Him to visit!"[18] Muriel left The Kilns a year later after getting "odder and odder."[19] Jack concluded that even if she weren't actually insane, her temperament would work against any happiness she might have. He felt deeply sorry for her.

On December 20, Jack wrote to Arthur Greeves that Mrs. Moore's varicose ulcer was getting "worse and worse," and domestic help was harder to get. "Sometimes I am very unhappy, but less so than I have often been in what were (by external standards) better times."[20]

He conceded—as he had observed through Screwtape in *The Screwtape Letters*—that all the annoying interruptions weren't actually interruptions of "one's 'own', or 'real' life" but *are* real life—the "life God is sending one day by day: what one calls one's 'real life' is a phantom of one's own imagination." It was difficult for Jack to be patient or provide sympathy. His "stock of love" seemed inadequate at such times.[21]

Jack had also been busy with other writing, finishing *That Hideous Strength*, the third installment of his science fiction trilogy, as well as his usual duties with the college, RAF, and volunteer work.

How Jack had written the BBC scripts at all, if a couple of weeks late, is a mystery.

❈ ❈ ❈

An associate producer of Fenn's read Jack's seven new scripts and reported that they were "up to standard" and "one just has to take one's hat off to them."[22]

Fenn wrote to commend Jack for his work. Once again he had "achieved a quite astonishing degree of clarity in a very difficult subject."[23] The analogies needed some "scrutiny," Fenn said, but the bigger worry was the length of each script. Jack had written *ten*-minute scripts, in deference to the timing of the last series, but this one needed *fifteen*-minute scripts. At least the error was caught earlier this time. Fenn asked if Jack could add to them; if rewriting wasn't possible, Fenn offered to give the five minutes away to another program.

Jack was agreeable to doing whatever was necessary once he saw the typed copies. He took an amused view of Fenn's "threatened 'scrutiny.' " of his analogies, observing that the word itself had a "sinister sound suggesting Scrooge, screws, Screwtape, scraping, and Inland Revenue."* Jack then insisted that Fenn come to Oxford to dine and perhaps spend the night for his "screw-tiny."[24]

---

* The British version of the Internal Revenue Service.

Fenn sent Jack the typed manuscripts along with detailed suggestions about their lengths and three pages of comments. It was indicative of his comfort with Jack and the mutual respect they had for each other by that time.[25]

Jack challenged some of Fenn's suggestions—in one case, in the final talk called "New Men," about how to best use biological organisms as an analogy, and in another, because going on too long about the church might raise denominational issues. Otherwise, he promised to press on.

The new year of 1944 found Jack completing the scripts. On January 9, Jack presented Fenn with a few title suggestions for the series, including the following:

"What Christians think God is like"

"What is God like: The Christian answer"

"Beyond Personality: or the Christian God"[26]

The BBC threw Jack another curve in early February when it slotted Jack's talks at the egregious hour of 10:20 p.m. Fenn, knowing how the change would affect Jack, argued with the powers that be why the time would be difficult and suggested as an alternative that they broadcast from Oxford. The powers that be refused. As a compromise they offered recording the series—though they disliked doing that, since it "always [dropped] the temperature in the audience."[27]

"Pox on your 'powers'!" Jack replied to Fenn on February 10. "Who the devil is going to listen to anything at 10:20?"[28]

Jack was prepared to cancel doing the program, suggesting they try again later in the year. But knowing Fenn wasn't likely to agree, he looked at his schedule and offered a counterproposal: he would do *three* live talks and catch the midnight train home (getting him to bed at three o'clock in the morning). The rest of the talks would have to be recorded.[29]

In case Fenn missed his irritation, Jack added, "If you know the address of any reliable firm of assassins, nose-slitters, garrotters and poisoners I should be grateful to have it. I shall write a book about the BBC—you see if I don't!"[30]

Fenn, in his reply on February 12, assured Jack that if he knew any assassins, nose-slitters, garrotters, and poisoners, he would have used them himself. He tried to assure Jack that the late hour often meant they would have a more intelligent audience. Fenn then offered a schedule that would allow Jack to record one talk before doing the live one, thus doubling what they could accomplish each time Jack came to London. Jack consented to the plan.

A final complication emerged during the series when Jack developed a cough—mentioned by Fenn in a letter dated February 28—and then Jack sent a telegram the following week saying that he would be unable to broadcast on March 7, as planned.

Jack's health, as would become evident later, would suffer from his relentless schedule.

❊ ❊ ❊

Beyond Personality was substantially different from Jack's previous three series, going yet further into the theological territory he had avoided previously. He determined that his audience should be able to handle the subject matter with intelligence. "You're not children: why should you be treated like children?" he asked.[31] He then proceeded with candid talks about the importance of theology, not as a replacement for experience, but to give experience a deeper context.

"Theology is practical," Jack said.[32] From there, the first talk[33] delved into the Christian concept of "becoming" children of God* and the difference between *begetting*, which is a sense of reproduction (humans beget humans, birds beget birds, etc.) versus *making*, which is an act of creation (humans make statues, birds make nests, etc.). The difference is important as we come to understand the physical life (using the Greek word *Bios*) and the spiritual life (*Zoe*). Christianity, he concluded, is like looking at our world as a great sculptor's shop. "We are the statues and there is a rumour going round the shop that some of us are some day going to come to life."[34]

Having laid that foundation, Jack then moved on to "The Three-Personal God."[35] He described the Trinity as the three-person God, personal yet mysteriously "beyond personality"— not impersonal but *more* than a person. He contrasted the Christian view of God with the view that suggests humans are absorbed into God after death, which eliminates the existence of the one absorbed. Instead, Jack used the three dimensions of space to illustrate the Christian view of God: the basic human level (one separate human, another separate human) and the level of God, in which three persons exist just as a cube is six squares yet still one cube.

Jack then examined how we, as humans, can relate to those three persons, and how they relate to us—which is, in essence, *theology*. But all our theology is no good if God doesn't want to be known or, if He allows Himself to be known, is dependent on our condition (light is reflected better in a clean mirror rather than a dirty one). God desires to show Himself to "*real* men," those who aren't necessarily "individually good"[36] but united in a body, playing instruments in the same band, or like "organs in one body."[37]

It should be noted that in the published version of these

---

* and daughters

talks, Jack added an entire chapter exploring the nature of time in relation to God—namely, that God is *outside* of time as we know it, which means He isn't bound as we are to time but is able to answer prayers and deal with creation much like an author can give great care and attention to an individual character and her actions in a novel without the character being aware of the author's presence. (Jack admitted that it wasn't a perfect illustration, but it was a glimpse of the truth.) Here he also tackled God's knowledge of the future over and against our free will, explaining how, because God is outside of time, He sees past, present, and future as an ongoing reality—not as someone who experiences the past, present, and future as we do.

"Good Infection," the third talk,[38] explained the relationships of God as three persons—specifically, God and Jesus as Father and Son, with the third person, the Holy Spirit, being harder for most people to grasp, since He actually lives inside us and works through us, making possible a life that serves as a "good infection."[39]

To help listeners understand all this talk of God's love, Jack clarified the various misconceptions of the phrase *God is love* and defined it as "the living, dynamic activity of love" that "has been going on in God forever and has created everything else."[40] The point, then, is that "every Christian is to become a little Christ. The whole purpose of becoming a Christian is simply that: nothing else."[41]

In the next talk, "The Obstinate Toy Soldiers,"[42] Jack returned to the concept of "becoming" sons of God and the obstacles to that happening. Using tin soldiers as his word picture, he demonstrated how God had to become a man in order live, die, and come alive again to show what all human beings were meant to be. He conceded that the illustration, like most illustrations, reached a breaking point, but the word picture served its purpose.

The published version of the talks added three chapters, the first called "Two Notes" to respond to questions Jack had received about his obstinate toy soldiers and his statement that the whole human race was like an organism.[43]

Jack used two fairy tales at the start of the fifth talk, called "Let's Pretend,"[44] to move listeners from the facts about God to see what difference all this "Theology" made. With the first story of "Beauty and the Beast," he reminded listeners about a girl treating a monster like a human, which it eventually became. With the second story, he told of a man who was so ugly that he wore a beautiful mask. After years, unbeknownst to him until he took the mask off, his face had conformed to the shape of the mask and was beautiful. Jack invited his listeners to "pretend," not as a pretense to replace something real, but as if they were something they hadn't become, much as children pretend to be grown-ups or soldiers. In a sense, he wanted his listeners to *practice* being like Christ, with the idea that God, inside of them, would make that a reality. Then, as genuine "carriers" of Christ, they would spread the "good infection" to others.[45]

"Is Christianity Hard or Easy?"[46] wasn't a trick question Jack posed in his sixth talk, but a thoughtful devotional about the difficulties of following Christ. He looked candidly at the relationship between our efforts at "being good" and the work God must do in us—thoroughly, without reservations or conditions. That's the "whole of Christianity": yielding fully to God to do what He must with us. Extending beyond an individual experience, Jack asserted that the church "exists for nothing else but to draw men into Christ, to make them little Christs. If they're not doing that, all the cathedrals, clergy, missions, sermons, even the Bible itself, are simply a waste of time."[47]

The other two chapters Jack added for the published version dealt with "Counting the Cost," which addressed responses to the previous talk about Christianity, and "Nice People or New Men," which dug deeper into becoming "perfect" as God is perfect (being turned from "a horse into a winged creature"). He also used the opportunity to explore the meaning of redemption and what it is to be "nice." (This chapter would prove to be substantially longer than all the others.)[48]

The seventh talk, "The New Man,"[49] picked up on the idea of a horse turning into a winged creature, equating it with a spiritual form of evolution as Christians are meant for the "Next Step"—a change in an unexpected and different direction (not natural but coming from something outside nature). Christ Himself is that next step, the New Man, who spreads the "good infection" to those who have personal contact with Him. These "new men" in Christ are "dotted here and there all over the earth,"[50] recognizable if you know what to look for. In a fascinating way, these new men ought to be all alike, yet they aren't. The closer each man gets to taking *himself* out of the way for Christ to work, the more truly Christ makes the man become *himself.*

In conclusion Jack invited his listeners to give themselves up to find their real selves; submit to the death of their desires, even their bodies, to find eternal life. "Keep *nothing* back. Nothing that you have not given away will ever be really yours. Nothing in you that has not died will ever be raised from the dead. Look for yourself, and you will find in the long run only hatred, loneliness, despair, rage, ruin and decay. But look for Christ and you will find Him, and with Him everything else thrown in."[51]

✳   ✳   ✳

This time the BBC magazine the *Listener* published the scripts after they aired.[52] The advantage for Jack was that any letters printed there could be answered by him and, hopefully, reduce the number of the individual letters he'd get at home. Unfortunately, his hope wasn't realized. The mail continued to pour in, to the degree that Warnie began to catalog and number Jack's responses.

For Jack, the final series of talks was less convenient and more exhausting than the previous three. It seemed beset by annoying little problems that added a certain angst for Jack.

That didn't stop Welch and Fenn from offering him more opportunities—for *The Anvil*, for one-off topics, for another series on anything he wanted to discuss. Other broadcasters contacted him. One persistent Australian broadcaster tried to persuade Jack to redo his original talks for them. He refused, explaining that he simply couldn't go over the material and make it fresh. The producer persisted, offering other ideas. Jack refused again and again, finally stating that he couldn't do his best work presenting an idea that wasn't his.[53] Eventually the producer got the message.

After several refusals from Jack, Welch reluctantly removed Jack from the BBC religious programming lineup. In a letter dated November 22, 1945, Welch graciously wrote, "We should like you to know that whenever you feel you have something you very much want to say which should be said in front of the microphone, we should always be anxious to make space for you in our religious talks programme. It is some time since we had a series of broadcast talks from you, and a great many listeners are anxious to hear you again. . . . Do please feel free to put up ideas to us whenever they come to you."[54]

On October 9, 1944, *Beyond Personality: The Christian Idea of God* landed on store bookshelves—a final commemorative of the original broadcast talks.

It would be several years before Jack would look at that material again.

✻ ✻ ✻

The Reverend Dr. James Welch left his position as director of religious broadcasting to work part-time in 1945. He also became chaplain to His Majesty King George VI. Eventually he accepted a position in Nigeria as professor of religious studies and vice principal of Ibadan University College (1950–1954).[55] While there he taught the acclaimed author of *Things Fall Apart*, Chinua Achebe, who called Welch "an extraordinary man."[56] A grammar school there is named after him. In the 1960s he returned to England to work with the training board of the Christian Missionary Society until his death in 1967.

Apart from his work with Jack, Eric Fenn helped create the morning feature *Lift Up Your Hearts* and the Sunday evening program *Think on These Things*. He left the BBC in 1945 and joined SCM Press as an assistant editor; then he returned to the BBC in 1947 to work for the Overseas Service. He later became a literary editor at the British and Foreign Bible Society. In 1957 he was appointed professor of Christian doctrine at the Selly Oak Colleges in Birmingham. He also became the moderator for the Presbyterian Church of England—remarkable since it was the first time the position had been given to someone who had never pastored a congregation or served as a missionary. Fenn retired from Selly Oak in 1967 and continued to work in areas of ecumenicalism and theology until his death in 1995.[57]

Jack would never work in radio with the two men again.

MIRACLES, NARNIA, AND *MERE CHRISTIANITY*

THE YEARS FOLLOWING THE *Broadcast Talks* saw Jack's prolific writing continue, along with the joys and tragedies of a life lived in the midst of domestic and social conflict.

The D-day landings on June 6, 1944, were the pivot point for Allied forces to drive back the Germans. Jack, like the rest of the nation, marveled at the turn in the war, allowing a genuine hope that they might win in the end.

Their hope was circumvented, though, as the V-1 rockets—known as "buzz bombs"—from Germany hammered London and other parts of England, killing more than 6,000 people, with approximately 18,000 injured.[1] By September, even as Paris and Brussels were liberated, the improved V-2 ballistic rockets rained anew on London—and continued to do so until the following spring. Hitler's last-ditch attempt to conquer the British killed more than 2,700 civilians and injured another 6,500.[2]

In 1944 Jack began writing *Who Goes Home?*—a work that would eventually be known as *The Grand Divorce* and then published in book form as *The Great Divorce: A Dream*. Based on the "mediaeval fancy of the Refrigerium, by which the lost souls have an occasional holiday in Paradise,"[3] the novel was a concept Jack had toyed with since 1933. Hints of it appeared in his poetry and the chapter on hell in *The Problem of Pain*.[4] Jack returned to it with great enthusiasm early in the spring and read it to the Inklings for their input. The book was finished and typed by his friend Barbara Wall by the end of July.

In September, Mrs. Moore had a stroke and lost the use of her left arm. She was restricted to bed for a while. Jack, who played nurse for her, believed she would make a full recovery "*this* time."[5]

Meanwhile, Jack encouraged Tolkien to stop dabbling and work on The Lord of the Rings in earnest, as they read through the work in progress. In a remarkable piece of correspondence to an American professor, Jack gave a candid assessment of Tolkien, calling him a "great man" whose published works "ought to fill a shelf by now: but he's one of those people who is never satisfied with a manuscript. The mere suggestion of publication provokes the reply 'Yes, I'll just look through it and give it a few finishing touches'—which means that he really begins the whole thing over again."[6]

Like *The Screwtape Letters*, *The Great Divorce* appeared in the *Guardian* in installments, fourteen in all, beginning November 10, 1944. Reader responses were similar to the appearance of *Screwtape* in those same pages a few years before, with both praise and criticism coming from all quarters. Some reviewers thought it was a natural follow-up to *Screwtape*, inasmuch as it explored the darker themes of human rationalization, if in a different setting.

On November 29, Jack celebrated his forty-sixth birthday. By early December, national confidence in the outcome of the war had increased to the point where the Local Defence Volunteers officially disbanded. Jack's tour of duty in Oxford was finished.

Warnie worked on a book he'd begun in 1942 about life in France during the reign of Louis XIV. He continued to serve as Jack's secretary when he didn't disappear to escape the tension at home or indulge in his drinking.

Maids came and went as Mrs. Moore's condition deteriorated. But her daughter, Maureen, now pregnant, came to stay at The Kilns until the baby was delivered early in January. By mid-March, Jack turned down an invitation to tour America, in part because he had his "very old invalid mother" to look after.[7]

✳ ✳ ✳

The war in Europe reached its climax at the end of April 1945 as the Americans and Soviets reached the Elbe River. Within days Hitler killed himself in a Berlin bunker along with his mistress-turned-newlywed, Eva Braun. The Allies pushed into Berlin, and at 2:41 a.m. on May 7, General Alfred Jodl, on behalf of Germany, agreed to an unconditional surrender. The surrender was officially recognized at 11:01 p.m. on May 8. Britain's six years of war finally ended.

The streets of Oxford were overrun with revelers. Jack "found it impossible to feel either so much sympathy with the people or so much gratitude to God as the occasion demanded." He felt "awed" by the "burden of our favours" for everyone dear to him who had escaped the war "by a series of Providences, some not far short of miracles."[8]

Perhaps the end of the war, and his thoughts about friends who'd survived and those who'd lost loved ones, caused him to think of the "New Creation"—new heavens, a new earth, the resurrection of the body—and "how we have neglected these doctrines."[9]

On the very day of his musings, one of his closest friends was rushed to the hospital.

✳ ✳ ✳

Jack had become friends with Charles Williams shortly after writing letters of mutual appreciation for each other's work back in 1936. Williams was an author, playwright, and poet—but his day job was at the Oxford University Press (OUP). With the outbreak of war, the OUP relocated from London to Oxford, putting Jack and Williams in close proximity for the next six years. Williams became a member of the Inklings. Not all of the members appreciated him as much as Jack. Tolkien, for one, was wary of his influence on Jack's thinking and writing. Some biographers believe that Tolkien was upset to have been displaced in Jack's affections by Williams.

Williams and Jack often met two or three times a week on their own. Jack also set Williams up as a lecturer at the university and drew him into his network of friends.

On May 10, 1945, Williams was seized with pain in his abdomen and was rushed to the Radcliffe Infirmary. His wife, Florence (nicknamed Michal), dashed from London to be with him. He was transferred to Acland Nursing Home, where surgeons operated on an acute intestinal obstruction. Jack had no idea how serious Williams's condition was. Williams knew— and had said as much to an acquaintance before going into the hospital.[10]

Just days later, on Tuesday, May 15, Jack was on his way to the usual Inklings meeting. He stopped by the infirmary to drop off a book for Williams and to carry any messages Williams might have for the group. Upon arrival he was informed that Williams had died.

Jack wrote later that it was news he couldn't have expected less than if he himself had died. Stunned, he walked the short distance to the Eagle and Child—"the very streets looked different"—and delivered the news to the assembled Inklings. It was such a shock that Jack had "some difficulty in making them believe or even understand what had happened."[11]

At home at 12:50 that day, Warnie answered the telephone to hear a woman's voice asking if he would deliver a message to Jack: Mr. Charles Williams died at Acland that morning. Warnie felt as if he had "slipped and come down on [his] head on the pavement." He mourned the loss of a friend with whom he'd spent many happy hours. "There will be no more pints with Charles: no more 'Bird and Baby': the blackout has fallen, and the Inklings can never be the same again," he wrote. "And so vanishes one of the best and nicest men it has ever been my good fortune to meet. May God receive him into His everlasting happiness."[12]

Warnie dealt with his grief by going out for a drink.

For Jack it was the greatest loss he'd experienced up to that time, including his own father's death. He wrote, on the day Williams was buried, that it was an "odd" experience that affirmed his belief in immortality beyond his expectations, making it "almost tangible." It released him from his "old feelings of . . . horror and disgust at funerals, coffins, graves" and of ghosts, since he would be "more pleased than afraid" if Williams showed up. He suffered pain from the loss, and "no mere depression."[13]

A Productive Period

Here is a list of Lewis's writings from 1938 to 1952:

Out of the Silent Planet (September 23, 1938)

Rehabilitations and Other Essays (March 23, 1939)

The Personal Heresy: A Controversy (April 27, 1939)

The Problem of Pain (October 18, 1940)

The Screwtape Letters (February 9, 1942)

Broadcast Talks (July 13, 1942)

A Preface to Paradise Lost: Being the Ballard Matthews Lectures Delivered at University College, North Wales, 1941 (October 8, 1942)

The Abolition of Man or Reflections on Education with Special Reference to the Teaching of English in the Upper Forms of School (January 6, 1943)

Christian Behaviour (April 19, 1943)

Perelandra: A Novel (April 20, 1943)

Beyond Personality: The Christian Idea of God (October 9, 1944)

That Hideous Strength: A Modern Fairy-Tale for Grown-Ups (August 16, 1945)

The Great Divorce: A Dream (January 14, 1946)

Miracles: A Preliminary Study (May 12, 1947)

Arthurian Torso, Containing the Posthumous Fragment of the Figure of Arthur by Charles Williams and a Commentary on the Arthurian Poems of Charles Williams (October 21, 1948)

Transposition and Other Addresses (Unconfirmed date, 1949)

The Lion, the Witch, and the Wardrobe: A Story for Children (October 16, 1950)

Prince Caspian: The Return to Narnia (October 15, 1951)

Mere Christianity (July 7, 1952)

Plus more than ninety published essays, articles, sermons, and critiques

Jack set to work on a tribute to Williams in the form of a book titled *Essays Presented to Charles Williams*. With an introductory reminiscence by Jack, as well as an essay on writing stories, the work included essays by Tolkien, Dorothy Sayers, Warnie, and others.

✳ ✳ ✳

Even as Jack dealt with the loss of Charles Williams, he was also putting together an anthology from the work of another of his heroes: George MacDonald. Jack had been deeply impacted by MacDonald's *Phantastes* and other fantasy novels. With the appearance of MacDonald as a character in *The Great Divorce*, it made sense for Jack to give him public exposure through a collection of quotes and excerpts. He finished the effort only a few days after the funeral for Charles Williams. Geoffrey Bles published the book at the end of the year.

✳ ✳ ✳

Jack also finished *That Hideous Strength*, the final book in his science fiction trilogy. Centered on a Tower of Babel idea, he described it as a modern fairy tale for grown-ups. After its release in August 1945, some reviewers considered it a Charles Williams novel as written by C. S. Lewis. Williams's influence was certainly pervasive, as Jack set the story in an everyday world with normal people rather than on another planet—something Williams often did in his novels. Critics weren't impressed, complaining about caricatured and unconvincing characters.[14] The influence of Williams took Jack a step away from his usual strengths.

In contrast, the critics decided the following January that Jack was in better form with the book version of *The Great Divorce*.

❋ ❋ ❋

Postwar England was, in many respects, harder and more austere than it had been during the war. The nation's resources were depleted by the six years of battle. Food rationing increased. Coal and electricity were depleted, leaving The Kilns and Jack's rooms at the college cold and uncomfortable. Photos of Jack during this period show him wearing dressing gowns *over* his regular clothes.

Mrs. Moore became harder to manage and, if such a thing were possible, made even more demands on Jack. By this time any support the household was given by evacuees (or June Flewett, who'd gone off to college) had ended. Warnie, to his regret, was in greater proximity to Mrs. Moore at home and found himself resenting her even more for her domination over his brother. He believed she was losing her mind, descending into bitterness and hatred. She had been "dying for years," he wrote in his journal, with little left but "the flame of greed and hate" burning brightly amid "white ash."[15]

The brothers had a respite when, in June 1946, they journeyed north again—this time to the University of St. Andrews in Scotland, where Jack was given an honorary doctor of divinity degree—a rare honor for a lay theologian. The university commended Jack for his achievements in writing and broadcasting, using "theological reflection and poetic imagination"[16] to produce works of excellence.

In contrast to the depressing nature of England, Scotland seemed like a land of plenty with "real porridge, . . . butter, edible sausages, toast, marmalade, coffee!"[17]

❋ ❋ ❋

Jack seized every new opportunity as it came, helping new ventures to promote the Christian faith (a start-up periodical) and, at the insistence of Dorothy Sayers,[18] writing the book that would become *Miracles*.

Yet Jack felt guilty whenever he had to leave Mrs. Moore, turning down requests so he could stay at her bedside. Increasingly in his letters he referred to her as his old and infirm mother, for whom help was hard to come by. In the spring, Mrs. Moore came down with pneumonia and was ill for several weeks. More often than not, she stayed in her room and ruled the house from there. Multiple times throughout the day, she would summon Jack from his writing to take care of a menial task—or to intercede between her and the maids.

To give the brothers a break, Maureen offered to switch houses. She would care for her mother at The Kilns while Warnie and Jack stayed at her home in Malvern. It was a relief but served to intensify Warnie's alienation. Returning was more than he thought he could bear. Instead, he took an extended holiday in Ireland.

While there he drank so heavily he had to be taken, unconscious, to Our Lady of Lourdes Hospital in Drogheda, a town north of Dublin.

The hospital wired Jack about Warnie's condition. Jack raced there to be at his side, staying for a week at a nearby hotel. Upon his release Warnie decided not to return to The Kilns yet and stayed in Ireland for another month. Sadly, it wouldn't be his only visit to Drogheda. It would eventually become his home away from home, and the nuns at the hospital became his good friends. Jack returned to The Kilns alone.

Warnie's bout of self-indulgence not only weighed on Jack emotionally and psychologically but practically. The letter-writing assistance Warnie had provided for Jack now consumed two to three hours of Jack's time each day. He responded not only to fans in Britain but to his growing audience in America after his books, including the older works, were released in the United States. He came to the attention of national periodicals, journals, and many academics who found in his writing a fresh new approach to old theological ideas. Jack heard from Christians and skeptics alike who sought advice or insights into spiritual matters.

His book *Miracles* was published in May 1947[19] in both Britain and America, to widespread acclaim. In September, *Time* magazine placed Jack on the cover and published an extensive article about his life and work.

As rationing in Britain took on new extremes, American fans came to Jack's aid, sending him food, paper, and supplies on a regular basis. Typically, Jack didn't keep these gifts for himself but would share them with the Inklings and anyone else he met who had need.

❋ ❋ ❋

Jack famously said that his fiction often began with seeing "pictures" in his head. One picture that stuck with him over many years was of a "[f]aun carrying an umbrella and parcels in a snowy wood."[20] At various times, in various ways, he tried to write a story about that picture, but with little success.

He had begun to have dreams involving a lion, and then "suddenly Aslan came bounding" into the story, and "once He was there He pulled the whole story together."[21]

Jack began working on *The Lion, the Witch, and the Wardrobe* in the summer of 1948. As a tribute to the children who had impacted his life during the war, he started the story with four children who were evacuated to the house of an old professor. There they encountered a wardrobe—and through the wardrobe an entirely different world.[22] This first story of Narnia, and the subsequent six to follow, consumed Jack's attention over the next two years. He originally envisioned the series as a trilogy comprised only of *The Lion, the Witch, and the Wardrobe*; *Prince Caspian*; and *The Voyage of the Dawn Treader*. One can read the end of the latter and feel its sense of completion. But the idea for *The Horse and His Boy* came, and he couldn't resist continuing on.

In early 1949, in the midst of Jack's work on the Narnia stories, Warnie had another binge with alcohol. Jack rushed him to the Acland Nursing Home in Oxford. Warnie would spend an entire month there.

It may be that Jack didn't understand how difficult it was for Warnie to live at The Kilns. He was depressed by its cold dreariness, as compared to the warmth and coziness of a nursing home. When he did return to The Kilns, he went in to Mrs. Moore to say hello and was "given a lecture on the extreme coal shortage, the iniquities of Betty [a housemaid], and an enquiry as to how long I proposed to stay cured this time." Back downstairs in the "refrigerated study," he knew he was "indeed 'home' again. Whether from cold, temper, depression, or all three, I had a shocking night, and when I tried to pray I found the line 'dead.'"[23]

✳ ✳ ✳

If such a thing was possible, Jack's workload increased. He now tutored students in pairs with the hope it would economize his time. It didn't. He took the unusual step of having another tutor assist, but that didn't help either, as he still gave each student as much time as needed academically and personally.

Tolkien saw a solution to Jack's problem. A Merton professorship of modern English literature became available, and Tolkien, as a professor of English by then, lobbied to have Jack placed alongside him. As a full-time professor, Jack would no longer have to tutor on a one-on-one basis.

Once again the ongoing prejudice against Jack for his public Christianity worked against him. The three other professors who had to agree to Jack's candidacy "felt he had not produced a sufficient amount of scholarly work," and "his election would lower the status of the professorship and even discredit the English School."[24]

Jack soldiered on but felt increasingly tired and discouraged. He began to feel as if his zeal for writing, even his talent, was in decline. He questioned whether or not he was still pleasing his readers. He felt old.[25]

In the summer of 1949, the weight of his overactivity hit Jack hard. He suffered from delirium, headaches, sore throats, high temperatures, and swollen glands. His doctor, "Humphrey" Havard, realized Jack couldn't get adequate care at The Kilns and took him by ambulance to Acland for rest and doses of penicillin.

The cause, to no one's surprise, was exhaustion. Havard sternly said that unless Jack took time off, at least a month away from home, he wouldn't be responsible for Jack's future health. Warnie, "sick with fright and savage with anger," went back to The Kilns to inform Mrs. Moore about Jack's condition and the cause of it. He frightened her enough that she agreed to his time away.[26]

Jack left the nursing home and made arrangements for a holiday in Ireland. He anticipated staying near Arthur Greeves, whom he hadn't seen in years. It seemed "too good to be true," he wrote to his old friend.[27]

And so it was.

Warnie, traumatized by the idea of looking after Mrs. Moore

and The Kilns while Jack was away, drank heavily again. Jack took him to the hospital, but the staff there said he was too far gone for them to be of help. After meeting with a mental specialist, Jack had Warnie moved to an asylum. From there Warnie eventually returned to Drogheda, staying from the middle of August to the end of September 1949.

Jack canceled his month-long holiday.

✳ ✳ ✳

Somehow—and it's anyone's guess how—Jack finished *The Lion, the Witch, and the Wardrobe* and *Prince Caspian* and began work on *The Voyage of the Dawn Treader*.

Warnie returned from Drogheda, if temporarily, and finally finished his first book, *The Splendid Century: Some Aspects of French Life in the Reign of Louis XIV*. He optimistically began a sequel, *The Sunset of the Splendid Century*.

American scholar Chad Walsh wrote a book about Jack called *C. S. Lewis: Apostle to the Skeptics*, which released in the autumn of 1949. A woman named Joy Davidman Gresham read it and contacted Walsh to talk about Jack. She had become a Christian because of his writings, she said, but still had questions about points he'd made. Walsh suggested Joy write to Jack directly and gave her the address.

On January 10, 1950, Jack received his first letter from Joy. She commended him for the impact his writing had had on her life. She also raised some theological arguments that Jack, in his reply, completely dismantled.

Joy didn't mind. On the contrary, she thought that "being disposed of so neatly by a master of debate, all fair and square— it seems to be one of the great pleasures of life."[28]

* * *

By late April 1950, the severity of Mrs. Moore's condition required her to be watched constantly. One night she fell out of bed three times. Jack could no longer care for her at The Kilns. He placed her in a nearby nursing home and visited her every day.

The expense of her care bit into Jack's budget. He sacrificially gave the money from his extracurricular writing and essays to those in need and couldn't bring himself to deprive them. So, to save money, he canceled the holiday he had postponed from the year before. "I hardly know how I feel," he wrote to Arthur Greeves, "relief, pity, hope, terror, & bewilderment have me in a whirl. I have the jitters!"[29]

With Mrs. Moore out of the house, Jack's overall sense of stress and anxiety subsided. Life at The Kilns became more pleasant. He began to walk again, which gave him much-needed exercise. By the end of the year, he had to admit that he felt "more physically comfortable and more psychologically harmonious" than he had for years.[30]

Meanwhile, *The Lion, the Witch, and the Wardrobe* was published in October. *Prince Caspian* and *The Voyage of the Dawn Treader* were completed, and Jack had begun writing *The Horse and His Boy* (though it would be published after *The Silver Chair*). *The Magician's Nephew* soon followed.

Feelings of exhaustion and talk of old age disappeared in this surge of creativity.

* * *

Mrs. Moore was comfortable at the nursing home, quaintly called Restholme, though she slipped into a delirious state. On one visit Warnie found her in tears and panicked because she thought her daughter, Maureen, had been killed. Maureen was alive and well, but it took Warnie a while to persuade the poor woman.

Jack equated this period of Mrs. Moore's life with "a quiet return to infancy."[31] He hoped to be at her bedside when the end came.

Mrs. Moore died on January 12, 1951, passing quietly around 5:00 p.m. She was buried three days later at Holy Trinity Church in Headington Quarry, in the same grave as Alice Hamilton Moore, the "other Mrs. Moore," who had lived in The Kilns's bungalow back in 1939.

Warnie wasn't able to attend the funeral because of the flu, but he observed in his journal that her death put an end to "the mysterious self imposed slavery in which [Jack] has lived for at least thirty years."[32]

In August Jack finally took his long-awaited holiday and traveled to Northern Ireland with Warnie for two weeks.

✳ ✳ ✳

In the autumn of 1951, Magdalen College gave Jack a year's sabbatical to work on volume 3 of the Oxford History of English Literature, which he took to calling "OHEL." It was a massive endeavor that would take him two years to write.

At year's end, Prime Minister Winston Churchill offered Jack the honor of receiving the Commander of the Order of the British Empire, an award given to British subjects who demonstrated chivalry and bravery outside of battle. Jack declined on the grounds that those who believed his writings were part of any particular political agenda would have their suspicions confirmed if he appeared on Churchill's "honours" list.[33]

✳ ✳ ✳

Since the war, Jack's broadcast talks had been available in Britain and America as three separate books: *Broadcast Talks, Christian Behaviour*, and *Beyond Personality*. Apart from a few revisions and additions to clarify his ideas, the books encompassed the unedited scripts and kept the conversational tone intact through the use of contractions and italics (to emphasize certain words or phrases the way Jack had said them in the broadcasts).

In 1952, with the encouragement of his publisher, Geoffrey Bles, Jack combined the three books into one. Jack called it *Mere Christianity*, a phrase he had picked up from seventeenth-century English Puritan and theologian Richard Baxter's *Saints' Everlasting Rest*. For Jack, it captured the overriding intention behind the original broadcast talks: to explore those things commonly believed by "nearly all Christians at all times."[34]

The book was a "revised and amplified" version that comprised a lengthy introduction explaining the history of the content, why he had included some theological points while leaving others out, and a reiteration that he was writing as a layman and not as a theologian or clergyman. To acknowledge the difference between the spoken and written word, he opted for this edition to eliminate the contractions and italics except in cases where it might cause confusion. Titles for various chapters were added or restored. Jack also changed lines to the past tense that had originally referenced the war with Germany in the present tense—or he eliminated the reference completely. He added sections to clarify points listeners and readers had missed over the previous decade.

Geoffrey Bles published the book on July 7, 1952. Macmillan followed with the American edition on November 11. In both countries the single edition found an entirely new audience, many who didn't know about or hadn't heard the original broadcast talks.

✳ ✳ ✳

It had been seven years since the end of the war and the remarkable circumstances that brought Jack Lewis, James Welch, and Eric Fenn together to create the groundbreaking broadcast talks.

Now published in one volume, Jack's work had the chance to demonstrate its power anew. Very quickly it became one of the best-selling and most significant, and referenced, works of apologetics in the twentieth century—against which most other works of that kind would be compared. His articulation of the person of Christ, of the Trinity, of moral law and the need for salvation, of the nature of time and eternity, and so many of the other topics became commonplace assumptions for the average Christian, as if they'd always been part of the collective faith. It would become hard to imagine giving a defense of the faith without quoting C. S. Lewis in some way. Such was the power of his work.

✳ ✳ ✳

Within two months of the publication of *Mere Christianity*, Jack met Joy Gresham for lunch at the Eastgate Hotel just across from Magdalen College. They would meet up twice again in November. Joy would also spend two weeks with Jack and Warnie over Christmas that year. Eventually Jack and Joy would marry, bringing him great happiness—and then great pain when she died in 1960. But that's another story for another time.

✳ ✳ ✳

The publication of *Mere Christianity* served as a punctuation mark to a remarkable chapter in the life of Jack Lewis. In that chapter he wrote five books exploring theology from a layman's point of view, three science fiction novels exploring the human condition from a scientific point of view, a fantasy and a children's series exploring faith from a storyteller's point of view, a collection of diabolical "letters" exploring the human condition and spirituality from a demon's point of view, and countless articles, essays, and letters that would defend all he believed as a Christian from a professorial point of view.

He also became the voice of Christianity during Britain's worst crisis.

In the midst of personal hardship, he proved himself to be a steadfast, loving, candid, loyal, insightful, and reliable friend and brother, and a living example for the faith he defended. His generosity and self-sacrifice were evident in everything he did.

It was a chapter of amazing inspiration, creativity, and productivity. Few writers could hope to accomplish as much in a lifetime, let alone thirteen years.

That chapter ended, but a new one began. In the next twelve years, he would see his series of novels for children become classics; he would abandon Oxford for Cambridge, where the stigma of his Christian faith wouldn't be held against him; he would write more books exploring very specific and personal spiritual themes; and, of course, he would become involved with a woman named Joy, who would take him deeply into life, love, suffering, and eternity.

✳ ✳ ✳

In July of 1963, Jack became ill—so ill that he was admitted to the Acland Nursing Home for a blood transfusion. His body had been failing him. He'd had ongoing problems with his kidneys, prostate, and bladder, along with a weakened heart.

Shortly after being admitted to the hospital at five o'clock on July 15, he suffered a heart attack and slipped into a coma.

Minto's daughter, Maureen, visited, as did Tolkien. Walter Hooper, a young American who'd arrived earlier in the summer and remained to serve as a secretary to Jack, stayed nearby. Warnie was in Ireland—recovering again—and knew nothing of his brother's condition. Everyone assumed it was the end of Jack's life. An Anglican priest performed extreme unction at 2:00 p.m. on July 16. An hour later Jack opened his eyes and asked for a cup of tea.

It was a brief recovery, and Jack knew it. He soon resigned his position at Magdalen College in Cambridge and was elected an honorary fellow. He arranged for the clearance of his rooms and the disposal of books and furniture at Cambridge. He began to refer to himself in his letters as an "extinct volcano."[35] And, as term began anew at the university, he observed that "term will never again begin for me."[36]

Returning to The Kilns, Jack needed a full-time nurse to care for him. Walter Hooper came to assist every day and eventually moved into The Kilns.

In a letter to Arthur Greeves written September 11, Jack lamented that although he was comfortable and cheerful, he was saddened by the thought that they would never meet again in this life. He was also disappointed that his brother hadn't returned from Ireland and was probably drinking himself to death. "Tho' I am by no means unhappy I can't help feeling it was rather a pity I did revive in July," he wrote. "I mean, having been glided so painlessly up to the Gate it seems hard to have it shut in one's face and know that the whole process must some day be gone thro' again, and perhaps far less pleasantly! Poor Lazarus! But God knows best."[37]

Finally, late in September, Warnie returned to The Kilns, and the brothers had time to themselves, as they'd had years before. "The wheel had come full circle," Warnie wrote. "Once again we were together in the little end room at home, shutting out from our talk the ever-present knowledge that the holidays were ending, that a new term fraught with unknown possibilities awaited us both."[38]

On Friday, November 22, Jack and Warnie had breakfast together, dealt with the day's letters, and did the crossword puzzle in the newspaper. The two had lunch together. After Jack nodded off in a chair, Warnie suggested he go to bed. Later in the afternoon, Warnie made a pot of tea and peeked in on his brother. Jack was comfortably settled in his bed but still sleepy. Warnie left him to rest. An hour and a half later, Warnie heard a crash from Jack's bedroom. Rushing in, Warnie found Jack lying at the foot of his bed. He was still breathing but, within a few minutes, stopped. Jack Lewis was dead.[39]

※ ※ ※

In the essay "The World's Last Night," Jack wrote about a servant in Shakespeare's *King Lear*—a man "who is such a minor character that Shakespeare [did] not given him even a name." Perhaps the man is merely the "First Servant." The main characters around him are executing their dastardly plans. "They think they know how the story is going to end," Jack observed, "and they are quite wrong." The servant, with "no such delusions" or "notion how the play is going to go," sees the horror of old Gloucester being cruelly blinded. He cannot stand by while it happens. "His sword is out and pointed at his master's breast in a moment." But then the servant is stabbed from behind and falls dead. "That is his whole part: eight lines all told," Jack concluded. "But if it were real life and not a play, that is the part it would be best to have acted."[40]

It is likely Jack had no idea of the legacy he'd created. That he'd become one of the foremost writers and Christian apologists of the twentieth century wasn't something he would have thought about. He once commented about being a writer people might read—and forget—in no time at all. Shortly before his death, he told Walter Hooper that his royalties would be nonexistent within three years.[41]

For Jack it was enough to have done his duty in the time he was given. It was enough to be the servant without a name.

To paraphrase Shakespeare through Hamlet: "He was a man, take him for all in all, we shall not look upon his like again."[42]

Acknowledgments

A WORK LIKE THIS COULD not be built without the foundation of hard work done by others. In this case, I am indebted to the masterful efforts of Walter Hooper, who valiantly researched and compiled C. S. Lewis's writings into published form. The same can be said for Justin Phillips, who dug deep into the BBC's archives to unearth information about the BBC and its relationship with Lewis. I shudder to think what it would have taken to create this book and the corresponding *Focus on the Family Radio Theatre* audio drama without their labors.

I must also express my gratitude to Doug Gresham, the guardian of his stepfather's legacy. He has been a great source of information, a wise advisor, and a kind friend.

At Focus on the Family, my appreciation goes to executive producer Dave Arnold, friend and kindred spirit; vice president Jim Mhoon; production engineer Chris Diehl; film producer Mitch Wright; director of publishing Larry Weeden; editor *par excellence* Marianne Hering; and the behind-the-scenes team who were involved in all aspects of the audio drama and this book. And, of course, my heartfelt thanks stretch across the ocean to Philip Glassborow, who remains a constant source of encouragement and friendship.

Laura Schmidt at the Marion E. Wade Center, Wheaton College, Illinois, gave her time and energy to my niggling questions, as did Katie Ankers at the BBC Written Archives in Caversham, England. Thank you both.

To my wife, Elizabeth, my son, Tommy, and daughter, Ellie—as always, my love and thanks for your love and patience while I do what I do for a living.

Grateful acknowledgment is made to the publishers and copyright holders for permission to reproduce their material here.

Any errors are mine alone and not those of the fine people I've mentioned above, or the great works or authors I consulted.

Notes

PROLOGUE

1. C. S. Lewis, *Surprised by Joy: The Shape of My Early Life* (New York: Harcourt, Brace, 1956), 196.
2. Douglas H. Gresham, *Lenten Lands: My Childhood with Joy Davidman and C. S. Lewis* (New York: Macmillan, 1988), 49.
3. Lewis, *Surprised by Joy*, 197.

CHAPTER 1

1. Harold Nicolson, diary entry, Monday, June 6, 1938, in *Diaries and Letters, 1930–1964*, ed. Stanley Olson (New York: William Collins and Sons, 1980), 127.
2. Winston Churchill, speech to the House of Commons, London, November 12, 1940, quoted in "Neville Chamberlain," Churchill Centre, http://www.winstonchurchill.org/learn/ speeches/speeches-of-winston-churchill/104-neville-chamberlain.
3. Ibid.
4. Jonathan V. Last, "History According to Harry: Appeasement Fails with Warlocks Too," Opinion, *Wall Street Journal*, July 15, 2005.
5. William L. Shirer, *Berlin Diary: The Journal of a Foreign Correspondent, 1934–1941* (New York: Knopf, 1941), 148.
6. Winston Churchill, quoted in *Churchill by Himself: The Definitive Collection of Quotations*, Richard Langword, ed. (New York: Random House, 2008), 258. For the entire speech, see Winston S. Churchill, "Broadcast to the United States and to London by Winston S. Churchill," October 16, 1938, The Churchill Center, accessed March 26, 2014, http://www .winstonchurchill.org/learn/speeches/speeches-of-winston -churchill/524-the-defence-of-freedom-and-peace.
7. "Neville Chamberlain: 'Peace for Our Time,'" September 30, 1938, "Sources of British History," Britannia Historical

Documents, accessed August, 6, 2013, http://www.britannia
.com/history/docs/peacetime.html.

8. Winston Churchill, speech to the House of Commons, London,
October 5, 1939, quoted in William L. Shirer, *The Rise and Fall
of the Third Reich: A History of Nazi Germany* (New York: Simon
and Schuster, 1960), 423.

9. William F. Deedes, *A.R.P.: A Complete Guide to Civil Defence
Measures* (London: *Daily Telegraph*, 1939).

10. Stephen Wade, *Air-Raid Shelters of World War II: Family Stories of
Survival in the Blitz* (South Yorkshire, England: Pen and Sword
Books, 2011), 19.

11. Norman Longmate, *How We Lived Then: A History of Everyday
Life During the Second World War* (London: Arrow Books, 1973),
121–22.

12. Quoted in Vera Lynn, *We'll Meet Again* (London: Sidgwick and
Jackson, 1994), 11.

13. James Welch, "Religious Broadcasting in Wartime," in *BBC
Year Book, 1945* (London: British Broadcasting Corporation,
1945), 41.

14. B. G. O. Ovririe, "A Brief History," Old Boys Association, James
Welch Grammar School Emevor, accessed August 6, 2013,
http://jwgsemevor.org/index.php?option=com_content&view
=article&id=2&Itemid=4.

15. Welch, "Religious Broadcasting in Wartime," *BBC Year Book
1945*, 41–43.

16. Asa Briggs, *The BBC: The First Fifty Years* (New York: Oxford
University Press, 1985), 232n.

17. Justin Phillips, *C. S. Lewis in a Time of War* (New York:
HarperCollins, 2002), 1.

18. Ibid., 2.

19. Letter from C. S. Lewis to Warren Lewis, September 2, 1939.
See Walter Hooper, ed., *The Collected Letters of C. S. Lewis,
vol. 2, Books, Broadcasts, and the War (1931–1949)* (New York:
HarperCollins, 2004), 271.

20. Ibid.

21. Ibid.

22. Ibid.

23. Clyde S. Kilby and Marjorie Lamp Mead, eds., *Brothers and Friends: The Diaries of Major Warren Hamilton Lewis* (New York: Harper and Row, 1982), 177.

24. Letter from C. S. Lewis to Warren Lewis, September 2, 1939, in Hooper, *Collected Letters*, 2:271.

25. Letter from C. S. Lewis to Warren Lewis, September 18, 1939. Ibid., 2:275.

26. Letter from C. S. Lewis to Warren Lewis, September 2, 1939. Ibid., 2:271.

27. Briggs, *The BBC: The First Fifty Years*, 175–76.

28. Tom Hickman, *What Did You Do in the War, Auntie?: The BBC at War, 1939–1945* (London: BBC Books, 1995), 9.

29. "The Story of BBC Television—Closedown," "The History of the BBC," BBC, accessed August 1, 2013, http://www.bbc .co.uk/historyofthebbc/resources/tvhistory/closedown.shtml.

CHAPTER 2

1. A. J. P. Taylor, *English History, 1914–1945* (Oxford: Oxford University Press, 1975), 120. See also Dmitri Jdanov et al., "Estimates of Mortality and Population Changes in England and Wales over the Two World Wars," *Demographic Research* 13, no. 6 (November 17, 2005): 389, http://www.demographic-research. org/volumes/vol13/16/13-16.pdf; John Keegan, *The First World War* (New York: Vintage, 2000), e-book, chap. 1.

2. Norman Longmate, *How We Lived Then: A History of Everyday Life During the Second World War* (London: Arrow Books, 1973), 60.

3. Raynes Minns, *Bombers and Mash: The Domestic Front, 1939–45* (London: Virago, 1980), 20.

4. Longmate, *How We Lived Then*, 52.

5. Minns, *Bombers and Mash*, 17–21.

6. Longmate, *How We Lived Then*, 70–73.

7. The stone came from Headington Quarry, near Jack's house.

8. Jack's room were officially called Staircase III, Number 3, New Buildings. See Walter Hooper, ed., *The Collected Letters of C. S. Lewis*, vol. 1, *Family Letters, 1905–1931*. (New York: HarperCollins, 2004), 650.

9. Paddy's formal name was Edward Francis Courtenay Moore (1898–1918).

10. Walter Hooper, *C.S. Lewis: A Complete Guide to His Life and Works* (New York: HarperCollins, 1996), 710.

11. Mrs. Moore's full name was Janie King Askins Moore (1872–1951).

12. C. S. Lewis, *Surprised by Joy: The Shape of My Early Life* (New York: Harcourt, Brace, 1956), 188, 195.

13. Hooper, *C.S. Lewis, A Complete Guide to His Life and Works*, 11.

14. Ibid.

15. Colin Duriez, *J. R. R. Tolkien and C. S. Lewis: The Story of Their Friendship* (Phoenix Mill, UK: Sutton, 2003), 22.

16. Jack's letters reference other evacuees by the names of Annamarie and Sheila Morrison. Margaret Leyland identified herself as an evacuee and later told of her experiences at The Kilns in the Southern California C. S. Lewis Society's publication *The Lamp-Post*, no. 3 (July 1977).

17. Letter from C. S. Lewis to Warren Lewis, September 10, 1939, in Walter Hooper, ed., *The Collected Letters of C. S. Lewis*, vol. 2, *Books, Broadcasts, and the War, 1931–1949* (New York: HarperCollins, 2004), 273. The reference to "Henty" is author George Alfred Henty (1832–1902). He was best known for his many books and stories for boys.

18. Some of this information came courtesy of a letter from evacuee Margaret Leyland in the Southern California C. S. Lewis Society's publication *The Lamp-Post*, no. 3 (July 1977). Margaret lived at The Kilns from January to June 1940.

19. Letter from C. S. Lewis to Warren Lewis, September 10, 1939, in Hooper, *Collected Letters*, 2:273.

20. Ibid.

21. Letter from C. S. Lewis to Warren Lewis, September 18, 1939. Ibid., 2:277.

22. Letter from C. S. Lewis to Warren Lewis, September 10, 1939. Ibid., 2:273.

23. Letter from C. S. Lewis to Warren Lewis, September 18, 1939. Ibid., 2:276.

24. Patricia Heidelberger, quoted in Stephen Schofield, ed., *In Search of C. S. Lewis* (South Plainfield, NJ: Bridge Publishing, 1983), 53–54.

25. Letter from C. S. Lewis to Warren Lewis, September 18, 1939, in Hooper, *Collected Letters,* 2:277.

26. George Sayer, *Jack: C. S. Lewis and His Times* (New York: Harper and Row, 1988), 188.

CHAPTER 3

1. Neville Chamberlain, radio address, London, September 3, 1939; see "The Transcript of Neville Chamberlain's Declaration of War," BBC Archive, accessed August 13, 2013, http://www.bbc .co.uk/archive/ww2outbreak/7957.shtml?page=txt.

2. Neville Chamberlain, radio address, London, September 3, 1939; see "The Transcript of Neville Chamberlain's Declaration of War," "Archive," BBC, accessed March 13, 2014, http://www .bbc.co.uk/archive/ww2outbreak/7957.shtml?page=txt.

3. Joseph Macleod, quoted in Philip Ziegler, *London at War, 1939– 1945* (New York: Knopf, 1995), 38.

4. Norman Longmate, *The Home Front: An Anthology of Personal Experience, 1938–1945* (London: Chatto and Windus, 1981), 25–26.

5. *Reader's Digest Illustrated Story of World War II* (Pleasantville, NY: Reader's Digest Association, 1969), 67.

6. Eric Fenn noting James Welch's approach, interview by Frank Gillard, July 4, 1986, in "BBC History: Religious Broadcasting," BBC Oral History archive, 2.

7. James Welch, "Religious Broadcasting in Wartime," *BBC Year Book 1945,* 41–42.

8. Keith Clements, *Oxford Dictionary of National Biography* (Oxford: Oxford University Press, 2004–2013), s.v. "Fenn, (John) Eric," http://www.oxforddnb.com/view/printable /101335.

9. Welch, "Religious Broadcasting in Wartime."

10. Ibid.

11. Ibid.

12. Ibid.

13. J. C. W. Reith, *Broadcast over Britain* (London: Hodder and Stoughton, 1924), 17.

14. "Broadcasting House: What to See Inside," "About the BBC," BBC, accessed March 14, 2014, http://www.bbc.co.uk/broad castinghouse/visitorinformation/whattoseeinside.html.

15. Ibid.; reference to the Latin inscription in Lyndon Bowring, "The Tide of Secularisation," *Revival Times* 8, no. 5 (May 2006), http://www.revivaltimes.org/index.php?aid=1045.

16. Robert Beaken, *Cosmo Lang: Archbishop in War and Crisis* (New York: I.B. Tauris, 2012), 187.

17. Eric Fenn, interview by Frank Gillard, July 4, 1985, "BBC History: Religious Broadcasting," BBC Oral History archive, 3–4.

18. Beaken, *Cosmo Lang*, 187.

19. Eric Fenn, interview by Frank Gillard, July 4, 1986, BBC Oral History archive, 4.

CHAPTER 4

1. Letter from C. S. Lewis to Warren Lewis, September 10, 1939, in Walter Hooper, ed., *The Collected Letters of C. S. Lewis*, vol. 2, *Books, Broadcasts, and the War, 1931–1949* (New York: HarperCollins, 2004), 272.

2. Letter from C. S. Lewis to Eliza Butler, October 14, 1940. Ibid., 2:448.

3. Ibid.

4. Joseph Arthur Greeves (1895–1966) was Jack's boyhood friend from Belfast, Ireland.

5. Letter from C. S. Lewis to Arthur Greeves, December 27, 1940, cited in Walter Hooper, ed., *They Stand Together: The Letters of C. S. Lewis to Arthur Greeves, 1914–1963* (New York: Macmillan, 1979), 487.

6. Letter from C. S. Lewis to Warren Lewis, September 18, 1939. Hooper, *Collected Letters*, 2:275.

7. Letter from C. S. Lewis to Warren Lewis, September 10, 1939. Ibid., 2:273.

8. Vera Lynn, *We'll Meet Again* (London: Sidgwick and Jackson, 1994), 109.

9. Frederick William Calcutt Paxford (1898–1979); see Hooper, *Collected Letters*, 2:213.

10. Letter from C. S. Lewis to Arthur Greeves, March 28, 1937. Ibid., 2:213.

11. Douglas H. Gresham, *Lenten Lands: My Childhood with Joy Davidman and C. S. Lewis* (New York: Macmillan, 1988), 98.

12. Fred Paxford, quoted in Walter Hooper, *Past Watchful Dragons: The Narnian Chronicles of C. S. Lewis* (New York: Collier, 1979) 6, cited in Walter Hooper, *C. S. Lewis: A Companion and Guide* (New York: HarperCollins, 1996), 717.

13. "Siege Cake" recipe, adapted from Raynes Minns, *Bombers and Mash: The Domestic Front, 1939–45* (London: Virago, 1980), 126.

14. Justin Phillips, *C. S. Lewis in a Time of War* (New York: HarperCollins, 2002), 175.

15. Norman Longmate, *How We Lived Then: A History of Everyday Life During the Second World War* (London: Arrow Books, 1973), 141.

16. Letter from C. S. Lewis to Arthur Greeves, September 15, 1939. Hooper, *Collected Letters*, 2:274.

17. Ibid.

18. William F. Deedes, *A.R.P.: A Complete Guide to Civil Defence Measures* (London: *Daily Telegraph*, 1939), 69.

19. Letter from C. S. Lewis to Warren Lewis, September 10, 1939. Hooper, *Collected Letters*, 2:273.

20. Douglas Gresham, correspondence with the author, June 2013.

CHAPTER 5

1. Letter from C. S. Lewis to Warren Lewis, September 18, 1939. Walter Hooper, ed., *The Collected Letters of C. S. Lewis*, vol. 2, *Books, Broadcasts, and the War, 1931–1949* (New York: HarperCollins, 2004), 2:276.

2. Lester J. Barston and Josephine B. Curry, *In the Shadow of the Hawk: An Intimate Chronicle of World War II and One Woman's Search for Meaning*, (Lanham, MD: University Press of America, 2004), 119.

3. Asa Briggs, *The BBC: The First Fifty Years* (New York: Oxford University Press, 1985), 175.

4. Ernest Newman of the *Sunday Times*, quoted in Briggs, *The BBC: The First Fifty Years*, 177.

5. Letter from C. S. Lewis to Warren Lewis, November 5, 1939. Mrs. Alice Hamilton Moore (1853–1939). Hooper, *Collected Letters*, 2:281.

6. Ibid.

7. Letter from C. S. Lewis to Warren Lewis, November 11, 1939. Ibid., 2:287.

8. C. S. Lewis, *The Problem of Pain* (London: Centenary Press, 1940), vii.

9. Scholar Devin Brown in *A Life Observed: A Spiritual Biography of C.S. Lewis* ([Grand Rapids: Brazos Press, 2013], 111–12) points out that both Jack and Warnie had inherited genetically defective thumbs from their father. They couldn't bend the joint farthest from the nail, which impeded their ability to play most sports.

10. Kathryn Lindskoog, *C. S. Lewis: Mere Christian* (Wheaton, IL: Shaw, 1987), 12.

11. C. S. Lewis, *Surprised by Joy: The Shape of My Early Life* (New York: Harcourt, Brace, 1956), 133.

12. George MacDonald (1824–1905).

13. Gilbert Keith Chesterton (1874–1936) was a Catholic essayist, novelist, poet, and Christian apologist.

14. Lewis, *Surprised by Joy*, 210.

15. C. S. Lewis, quoted in George Sayer, *Jack: C. S. Lewis and His Times* (New York: Harper and Row, 1988), 132.

16. Lewis, *Surprised by Joy*, 228–29.

17. John Ronald Reuel Tolkien (1892–1973) was a close friend of Jack Lewis and a member of the Inklings. He is best known as the author of *The Hobbit* and The Lord of the Rings, but he was also a university professor, philologist, and poet.

18. Henry "Hugo" Victor Dyson (1896–1975) was an English academic who taught first at the University of Reading and later became a fellow and tutor at Oxford's Merton College. He was a member of the Inklings.

19. Lewis, *Surprised by Joy*, 237.

20. Ibid.

21. James Welch, quoted in Tom Hickman, *What Did You Do in the War, Auntie?: The BBC at War, 1939–1945* (London: BBC Books, 1995), 87.

22. Briggs, *The BBC: The First Fifty Years*, 187.

23. Hickman, *What Did You Do in the War, Auntie?*, 87.

24. Briggs, *The BBC: The First Fifty Years*, 186–87.

25. The Inklings unofficially began in 1929 when Lewis and Tolkien met to read their works to each other. A couple of years later, one of Jack's undergraduate students formed a literary club for reading, review, and discussion, which he called the "Inklings." Jack and Tolkien were invited to the meetings, presumably to give them credibility and permanence. After the initial group of students moved on, Lewis and Tolkien retained the name for their get-togethers.

26. Letter from C. S. Lewis to Arthur Greeves, November 8, 1931. Hooper, *Collected Letters*, 2:13.

27. Ibid.

28. Ibid.

29. Ibid.

30. Owen Barfield (1898–1997) was a literary and philosophical academic and author but made his principal living as a lawyer. Lewis wrote that Barfield was "the wisest and best of my unofficial teachers" (*The Allegory of Love: A Study in Medieval Tradition* [London: Oxford University Press, 1959], dedication).

31. Robert Emlyn Havard (1901–1985) was Lewis's doctor, a member of the Oxford University Socratic Club. Havard met Lewis in 1934 while treating him for influenza. The two men spent only five minutes on Jack's condition and then spun off into a lengthy conversation about ethics and philosophy. Havard described this meeting in his essay "Philia: Jack at Ease," in James T. Como, ed., *C. S. Lewis at the Breakfast Table and Other Reminiscences* (New York: Macmillan, 1979).

32. Nevill Henry Kendal Aylmer Coghill (1899–1980) met Lewis as a fellow student in 1923. Lewis described him as "the most intelligent and best-informed man in that class" and was shocked to discover that he was a Christian (*Surprised by Joy*, [New York: Harcourt, Brace, 1956], 212). Coghill was renowned as a scholar of Middle English literature and acclaimed for his Chaucerian poetry. He was also a producer for the Oxford University Dramatic Society and "discovered" the actor Richard Burton.

33. Charles Lesley Wrenn (1895–1969) was Lecturer in English Language at Oxford, and later, a Rawlinson and Bosworth Professor of Anglo-Saxon at Oxford University.

34. Charles Walter Stansby Williams (1886–1945) was an author, playwright, poet, lecturer, tutor, and editor for the Oxford University Press (OUP) from 1908 until his sudden death in May 1945. Williams and Lewis became friends after an exchange of letters expressing mutual respect for each other's works. The war forced the OUP to move from London to Oxford. Lewis wrote, "We met one another about twice a week, sometimes more" (C. S. Lewis, ed., *Essays Presented to Charles Williams* [Grand Rapids, Eerdmans, 1966], viii).

35. Letter from C. S. Lewis to Arthur Greeves, November 8, 1931. Hooper, *Collected Letters*, 2:13.

36. Ibid., 14.

37. Letter from C. S. Lewis to Warren Lewis, November 5, 1939. Hooper, *Collected Letters*, 2:282.

38. Ibid., 2:283.

39. Letter from C. S. Lewis to Warren Lewis, September 10, 1939. Ibid., 2:272.

40. Letter from C. S. Lewis to Dom Bede Griffiths, January 17, 1940. Ibid., 2:327.

41. Letter from C. S. Lewis to Warren Lewis, February 18, 1940. Ibid., 2:350.

42. Ibid.

43. Karl Barth (1886–1968) was a Protestant theologian who studied, pastored, and taught in Germany. In 1935 he was ejected by the University of Bonn faculty because he resisted the German National Socialist movement.

44. Letter from C. S. Lewis to Warren Lewis, February 18, 1940. Hooper, *Collected Letters*, 2:351.

45. Letter from C. S. Lewis to Warren Lewis, February 18, 1940. Hooper, *Collected Letters*, 2:350.

46. Ibid.

47. Ibid.

48. Como, *C. S. Lewis at the Breakfast Table*, 195.

49. Ibid., 2:351–52.

50. Letter from C. S. Lewis to Warren Lewis, March 21, 1940. Ibid., 2:368–69.

51. Letter from C. S. Lewis to Sister Penelope CSMV, November 8, 1939. Ibid., 2:285.

52. Letter from C. S. Lewis to Warren Lewis, September 10, 1939. Ibid., 2:272.

53. Letter from C. S. Lewis to Warren Lewis, December 3, 1939. Ibid., 2:302.

54. Ibid.

55. Lewis, *The Problem of Pain*, 93.

56. C. S. Lewis, *God in the Dock: Essays on Theology and Ethics* (Grand Rapids: Eerdmans, 1970), 98.

CHAPTER 6

1. Richard Collier, *1940: The World in Flames* (London: Hamish Hamilton, 1979), 3.
2. Ibid.
3. Louis L. Snyder, *Encyclopedia of the Third Reich* (New York: McGraw-Hill, 1976), 217.
4. Ibid., 217.
5. Ibid., 187, 228.
6. Leonard Mosley et al., *Battle of Britain* (Alexandria, VA: Time-Life Books, 1977), 48.
7. Snyder, *Encyclopedia of the Third Reich*, 217.
8. Mosley, *Battle of Britain*, 49.
9. Collier, *1940: The World in Flames*, 4.
10. Ibid.
11. Ibid., 26.
12. Ibid., 12.
13. Information on German troop movements in Norway and Denmark from Collier, *1940: The World in Flames*, 34–35.
14. Ibid., 35–36.
15. Ibid., 36.
16. Gerda Haas, *Tracking the Holocaust* (Minneapolis: Runestone Press, 1995), 71; Nathan Miller, *War at Sea: A Naval History of World War II* (Oxford: Oxford University Press, 1995), 65.
17. James Welch, "Programme for the Forces: Religious Broadcasting; Report of Director of Religious Broadcasting on His Visit to the Western Front," April 1940, BBC Written Archives Centre (Caversham Park), R34/269/3/File 2.
18. Ibid.
19. Ibid.
20. Ibid.
21. Ibid.
22. Collier, *1940: The World in Flames*, 45.
23. Ibid.

24. Letter from C. S. Lewis to Warren Lewis, April 21, 1940, in Walter Hooper, ed., *The Collected Letters of C. S. Lewis*, vol. 2, *Books, Broadcasts, and the War, 1931–1949* (New York: HarperCollins, 2004), 400.

25. Collier, *1940: The World in Flames*, 46.

26. Ibid., 47.

27. Leo Amery, speech to the House of Commons, London, May 7, 1940, in "Leo Amery—1940 Speech in the House of Commons," UKpolitics.org, accessed January 1, 2014, http://www.ukpolitics. org.uk/node/354.

28. Letter from C. S. Lewis to Warren Lewis, March 17, 1940. Hooper, *Collected Letters*, 2:363.

29. Letter from C. S. Lewis to Warren Lewis, April 21, 1940. Ibid., 2:399.

30. Letter from C. S. Lewis to Arthur Greeves, May 9, 1940. Ibid., 2:413.

31. Information on Winston Churchill from *Reader's Digest Illustrated Story of World War II* (Pleasantville, NY: Reader's Digest Association, 1969), 118–19.

32. *Reader's Digest Illustrated Story of World War II*, 77.

33. General Maxime Weygand, quoted in Collier, *1940: The World in Flames*, 67.

34. "Dunkirk—a Few Facts," "Press Office," BBC Home, accessed February 4, 2013, http://www.bbc.co.uk/pressoffice/pressreleases /stories/2004/02_february/03/dunkirk_facts_figures.shtml.

35. Ibid.

36. Collier, *1940: The World in Flames*, 84.

37. Ibid., 88. See also "World War II: Dunkirk Evacuation," Desertwar.net, May 13, 2013, http://desertwar.net/dunkirk-evacuation.html.

38. Winston Churchill, "We Shall Fight on the Beaches," speech to the House of Commons, London, June 4, 1940, http://www .winstonchurchill.org/learn/speeches/speeches-of-winston -churchill/128-we-shall-fight-on-the-beaches.

39. Collier, *1940: The World in Flames*, 89.

40. Winston Churchill, "Their Finest Hour," speech to the House of Commons, London, June 18, 1940, http://www.winstonchurchill .org/learn/speeches/speeches-of-winston-churchill/1940-finest -hour/122-their-finest-hour.

41. *Front Line, 1940–1941: The Official Story of the Civil Defence of Britian* (London: H. M. Stationery Office, 1942), 6.

42. Letter from C. S. Lewis to Warren Lewis, July 20, 1940. Hooper, *Collected Letters*, 2:425.

43. Ibid., 2:426.

44. Ibid., 2:427.

45. Winston Churchill, "The Few," speech to the House of Commons, London August 20, 1940, http://www.winston churchill.org/learn/speeches/speeches-of-winston-churchill/113 -the-few.

46. Mosley, *Battle of Britain*, 117–18.

47. Ibid.

48. William L. Shirer, *Berlin Diary: The Journal of a Foreign Correspondent, 1934–1941* (New York: Knopf, 1941), 496.

49. Ibid., 496–97.

CHAPTER 7

1. Letter from C. S. Lewis to Warren Lewis, August 17, 1940, in Walter Hooper, ed., *The Collected Letters of C. S. Lewis*, vol. 2, *Books, Broadcasts, and the War, 1931–1949* (New York: HarperCollins, 2004), 434.

2. Ibid., 2:436.

3. The name *Bosphorus* came from a boat created by Jack and Warnie in the Boxen stories they wrote when they were children. It is also the name of the Istanbul Strait separating Asia and Europe.

4. Letter from C. S. Lewis to Arthur Greeves, May 25, 1941. Hooper, *Collected Letters*, 2:486.

5. George Sayer, *Jack: C. S. Lewis and His Times* (New York: Harper, 1988), 162.

6. Daniel Smith, *The Spade as Mighty as the Sword* (London: Aurum, 2011), 145–47.

7. Tom Hickman, *What Did You Do in the War, Auntie?: The BBC at War, 1939–1945* (London: BBC Books, 1995), 76.

8. Vera Lynn, *We'll Meet Again* (London: Sidgwick and Jackson, 1994), 133–34.

9. James Welch, *The BBC Handbook, 1942* (London: British Broadcasting Corporation, 1942), 59.

10. *Front Line, 1940–1941: The Official Story of the Civil Defence of Britian* (London: H. M. Stationery Office, 1942), 11; Richard Collier, *1940: The World in Flames* (London: Hamish Hamilton, 1979), 170. See also Winton G. Ramsey, ed., *The Blitz: Then and Now*, vol. 2, *September 1940–May 1941* (London: Battle of Britain Prints, 1988), 44–45.

11. *Front Line*, 12; Ramsey, *The Blitz: Then and Now*, 2:57.

12. Ramsey, *The Blitz: Then and Now*, 2:56–61; Collier, *1940: The World in Flames*, 171.

13. Donald Olson, Stephen Brewer, Donald Strachan, and Barry Shelby, *Frommer's Great Britain Day by Day* (Hoboken, NJ: John Wiley, 2012), 693.

14. Ibid., 194. See also, Justin Phillips, *C. S. Lewis and the BBC: Messages of Hope in the Darkness of War*, (London: HarperCollins, 2002), 70-2.

15. Asa Briggs, *The BBC: The First Fifty Years* (Oxford: Oxford University Press, 1985), 131n.

16. Hickman, *What Did You Do in the War, Auntie?*, 132.

17. Letter from C. S. Lewis to Douglas Bush, November 1, 1940. Hooper, *Collected Letters*, 2:452.

18. *"Id teneamus, quod ubique, quod semper, quod ab omnibus creditum est,"* from St. Vincent of Lérins, *Commonitorium*, chap. 4, sec. 3; see footnote 375 in Hooper, *Collected Letters*, 2:452.

19. Letter from C. S. Lewis to Mary Neylan, April 30, 1941. Hooper, *Collected Letters*, 2:482.

20. Ibid.

21. Letter from C. S. Lewis to Sister Penelope, November 4, 1940. Ibid., 2:453.

22. C. S. Lewis, *The Screwtape Letters,* annotated ed. *(New York: HarperCollins, 2013), xlii.*

23. Both essays are included in C. S. Lewis, *God in the Dock: Essays on Theology and Ethics,* ed. Walter Hooper (Grand Rapids: Eerdmans, 1970), 189–92, 193–95.

24. Walter Hooper, *C. S. Lewis: A Companion and Guide* (New York: HarperCollins, 1996), 803.

25. Information in this sidebar gleaned from Paul McCusker, "Introduction to the Annotated Edition" in Lewis, *Screwtape Letters,* annotated ed. See especially pages xix–xx.

26. Lewis, *Screwtape Letters,* 15, 61, 99, 156.

27. W. G. de Burgh, quoted in *Guardian,* November 22, 1940, in Walter Hooper, *C. S. Lewis: A Companion and Guide* (New York: HarperCollins, 1996), 302.

28. C. S. Lewis, ed., *Essays Presented to Charles Williams* (Grand Rapids: Erdmanns, 1966), xiii.

29. Charles Williams, review of *The Problem of Pain,* in *Theology* 42, no. 247 (January 1941), 62–63.

30. J. R. R. Tolkien, quoted in Colin Duriez, *J. R. R. Tolkien and C. S. Lewis: The Story of Their Friendship* (Phoenix Mill, UK: Sutton, 2003), 124.

31. C. S. Lewis, *Le Problème de la Souffrance,* trans. Marguerite Faguer (Bruges: Desclées de Brouwer, 1950), quoted in Hooper, *C. S. Lewis: A Companion and Guide,* 296–97.

CHAPTER 8

1. C. S. Lewis, *The Problem of Pain* (London: Centenary Press, 1940), 27–28.

2. Letter from James Welch to C. S. Lewis, February 7, 1941.

3. Ibid.

4. George Sayer, *Jack: C. S. Lewis and His Times* (New York: Harper and Row, 1988), 168.

5. Charles Gilmore, "To the RAF," in *C. S. Lewis at the Breakfast Table and Other Reminiscences,* James T. Como, ed. (New York: Macmillan, 1979), 187.

6. Winston Ramsey, ed., *The Blitz: Then and Now*, vol 2 (London: Battle of Britain Prints, 1988), 484.

7. Ibid., 2:485.

8. Norman Longmate, *How We Lived Then: A History of Everyday Life During the Second World War* (London: Arrow Books, 1973), 66.

9. Clyde S. Kilby and Marjorie Lamp Mead, eds., *Brothers and Friends: The Diaries of Major Warren Hamilton Lewis,* (New York: Harper and Row, 1982), 279.

10. John Ray, *The Night Blitz, 1940–1941* (London: Cassell, 1996), 227–32.

11. Letter from C. S. Lewis to Arthur Greeves, May 25, 1941. Hooper, *Collected Letters*, 2:486.

12. Letter from C. S. Lewis to Sister Penelope, May 15, 1941. Ibid., 2:485.

13. Ibid. Quoting the story of Balaam's ass from Numbers 22:24–31 in the Bible. Walter Hooper's note in *Collected Letters* (2:485) states that "beneath this letter Lewis drew a picture of a Balaam's Ass, flanked by a nun and a figure wearing a mortar-board. They are seated outside a stable in the radiance of a heavenly city."

14. Information in this sidebar from Walter Hooper, *The Collected Letters of C. S. Lewis*, vols. 1 and 2 (New York: HarperCollins, 2000, 2004), 1:993, 2:1055.

15. C. S. Lewis, *Surprised by Joy: The Shape of My Early Life* (New York: Harcourt, Brace, 1956), 130–31.

16. Charles Gilmore, "To the RAF," in *C. S. Lewis at the Breakfast Table*, 189.

17. Ibid.

18. Ibid., 188.

19. Longmate, *How We Lived Then*, 293.

20. Information in this sidebar from "Is Your Journey Really Necessary?," in Longmate, *How We Lived Then*, chap. 25.

21. Letter from C. S. Lewis to Arthur Greeves, May 25, 1941. Hooper, *Collected Letters*, 2:486.

22. Ramsey, *The Blitz: Then and Now*, 2:608–10.

23. Ray, *The Night Blitz*, 231.

24. Ibid., 231–32.

25. Ramsey, *The Blitz: Then and Now*, 2:626.

26. Letter from C. S. Lewis to Mary Neylan, October 2, 1941. Hooper, *Collected Letters*, 2:492.

27. "Learning in War-Time" was published in C. S. Lewis, *The Weight of Glory and Other Addresses* (New York: Macmillan, 1949), 43–54.

28. 2 Corinthians 4:17.

29. Eric Routley, quoted in Hooper, *Collected Letters*, 2:492.

30. C. S. Lewis, *The Weight of Glory and Other Addresses* (New York: Macmillan, 1949), 13.

31. Justin Phillips, *C. S. Lewis in a Time of War* (New York: HarperCollins, 2002), 92.

32. Ibid., 92.

33. Ibid., 114.

34. Ibid., 112, 114.

35. C. S. Lewis, *God in the Dock: Essays on Theology and Ethics,* ed., Walter Hooper (Grand Rapids: Eerdmans, 1970), 93.

36. Ibid., 98.

37. Ibid., 100.

38. Ibid., 101.

39. Ibid.

CHAPTER 9

1. Justin Phillips, *C. S. Lewis in a Time of War* (New York: HarperCollins, 2002), 119.

2. C. S. Lewis, *Broadcast Talks* (London: Geoffrey Bles, 1942), 9.

3. Ibid.

4. Ibid., 10.

5. In *C. S. Lewis in a Time of War*, Justin Phillips assembled the schedule from the BBC's *Radio Times* 72, no. 931

(August 1, 1941), which covered the programs for August 3–9, 1941.

6. Lewis, *Broadcast Talks*, 10.

7. Ibid., 13.

8. Ibid., 23.

9. Letter from Eric Fenn to C. S. Lewis, September 4, 1941.

10. C. S. Lewis, in *Broadcast Talks* script, August 20, 1941, BBC Written Archives Centre, Caversham, England.

11. Phillips, *C. S. Lewis in a Time of War*, 128.

12. Lewis, *Broadcast Talks*, 23–28.

13. Ibid., 27.

14. Ibid., 27–28.

15. Phillips, *C. S. Lewis in a Time of War*, 128.

16. Ibid.

17. Walter Hooper, *C. S. Lewis: A Companion and Guide* (New York: HarperCollins, 1996), 305. See also C. S. Lewis, *Broadcast Talks*, 26.

18. Letter from Eric Fenn to C. S. Lewis, August 21, 1941. See Phillips, *C. S. Lewis in a Time of War*, 124.

19. Lewis, *Broadcast Talks*, 29.

20. Ibid., 31.

21. Ibid., 32.

22. Ibid., 32.

23. Ibid., 33.

24. Undated postcard from C. S. Lewis to Eric Fenn, late August 1941. See Phillips, *C. S. Lewis in a Time of War*, 127.

25. Letter from Eric Fenn to C. S. Lewis, September 4, 1941, cited in Phillips, *C. S. Lewis in a Time of War*, 129.

26. John Lawler, interview by Walter Hooper, October 28, 1999, quoted in Phillips, *C. S. Lewis in a Time of War*, 119.

27. Letter from C. S. Lewis to Arthur Greeves, December 23, 1941. Hooper, *Collected Letters*, 2:504.

28. Letter from C. S. Lewis to Ronald Boswell (BBC), February 16, 1942. Ibid., 2:509.

29. Letter from C. S. Lewis to Eric Fenn (BBC), February 25, 1942. Ibid.

CHAPTER 10

1. Letter from C. S. Lewis to John Gordon Williams (BBC), September 30, 1941. Walter Hooper, ed. *The Collected Letters of C. S. Lewis*, vol. 2, *Books, Broadcasts, and the War, 1931–1949* (New York: HarperCollins, 2004), 491–92.

2. Letter from C. S. Lewis to Arthur Greeves, December 23, 1941. Ibid., 2:504.

3. Dorothy L. Sayers, *The Mind of the Maker* (New York: Harcourt, Brace, 1941), reviewed in *Theology* 43 (October 1941): 248–49.

4. J. W. Welch, foreword to *The Man Born to Be King* 2nd ed., by Dorothy L. Sayers (London: Victor Gollancz, 1957), 9.

5. Barbara Reynolds, "How Sayers Said It," *Church Times* (London), November 14, 1997.

6. Ibid. See also Welch, *The Man Born to Be King*, 9–10.

7. Reynolds, "How Sayers Said It."

8. Welch, in *The Man Born to Be King*, 15.

9. Hooper, *Collected Letters*, s.v. "Dorothy Sayers," 2:1070.

10. Information in this sidebar derived from Hooper, *Collected Letters*, s.v. "Dorothy Sayers," 2:1065–72.

11. Reynolds, "How Sayers Said It."

12. Letter from C. S. Lewis to Arthur Greeves, June 1, 1943. Hooper, *Collected Letters*, 2:580.

13. Letter to C. S. Lewis from Eric Fenn, December 5, 1941. See Justin Phillips, *C. S. Lewis in a Time of War* (New York: HarperCollins, 2002), 141.

14. James T. Como, *Remembering C. S. Lewis: Recollections of Those who Knew Him* (New York: Harcourt Brace, 1992), 246.

15. David Dimbleby and David Reynolds, *An Ocean Apart* (London: Hodder and Stoughton, 1988), 136.

16. *Reader's Digest Illustrated Story of World War II* (Pleasantville, NY: Reader's Digest, 1969), 25.

17. Information adapted from US War Department, *Over There: Instructions for American Servicemen in Britain, 1942*, Bodleian Library (Oxford: Oxford University Press, 1994).

18. Ibid., 10.

19. Ibid., 15.

20. Franklin D. Roosevelt cable to Winston Churchill, December 8, 1941, quoted in Dimbleby and Reynolds, *An Ocean Apart*, 137.

21. Winston Churchill, *The Second World War*, vol. 3, *The Grand Alliance* (New York: Houghton Mifflin, 1950), 540.

22. Broadcast on January 11, 1942, the first talk in series 2 was later titled "The Rival Conceptions of God." See C. S. Lewis, *Broadcast Talks* (London: Geoffrey Bles, 1942), 37–62.

23. Lewis, *Broadcast Talks*, 41.

24. Broadcast on January 18, 1942, the second talk was later called "The Invasion." See Lewis, *Broadcast Talks*, 41.

25. Ibid.

26. Broadcast on February 1, 1942, the third talk was later titled "The Shocking Alternative."

27. Lewis, *Broadcast Talks*, 47.

28. Ibid., 50.

29. Letter to C. S. Lewis from Eric Fenn, February 3, 1942. See Justin Phillips, *C. S. Lewis in a Time of War*, 149.

30. The fourth broadcast talk was later titled "The Perfect Penitent."

31. From the notes on the broadcast scripts. A similar quote can be found in Lewis, *Broadcast Talks*, 53.

32. The fifth talk broadcast February 15, 1942, and was later given the title "The Practical Conclusion."

33. Lewis, *Broadcast Talks*, 57.

34. Phillips, *C. S. Lewis in a Time of War*, 146.

35. The book was released in America more than a year later on February 16, 1943.

36. C. S. Lewis, *The Screwtape Letters* (London: Geoffrey Bles, 1942), ii.

37. Letter from C. S. Lewis to Eric Fenn, June 29, 1942. Hooper, *Collected Letters*, 2:522.

38. Jack's handwritten notes often included a variety of abbreviations—"wd" for "would," for example, and "Xtian" for "Christian."

39. Letter from C. S. Lewis to Eric Fenn, August 15, 1942. Hooper, *Collected Letters*, 2:528.

40. Letter from C. S. Lewis to Eric Fenn (BBC), November 30, 1942. *Collected Letters*, 2:538.

41. Ibid.

42. "The Three Parts of Morality" and "The Cardinal Virtues" comprised the first talk in series 3, *Christian Behaviour*, broadcast September 20, 1942.

43. C. S. Lewis, *Christian Behaviour* (London: Geoffrey Bles, 1943), 11–16.

44. The second talk broadcast September 27, 1942.

45. Jack would explore this idea even further in *The Great Divorce*.

46. Lewis, *Christian Behaviour*, 25.

47. The fourth talk broadcast October 11, 1942.

48. Lewis, *Christian Behaviour*, 26–27.

49. Ibid., 30–36.

50. The fifth talk broadcast October 15, 1942.

51. Lewis, *Christian Behaviour*, 37.

52. Information in this sidebar from Norman Longmate, "Eight Coupons for a Cassock," in *How We Lived Then: A History of Everyday Life During the Second World War* (London: Arrow Books, 1973), chap. 32.

53. Ibid., 388.

54. Ibid., 397.

55. The sixth talk in series 3, *Christian Behaviour*, broadcast October 25, 1942.

56. Lewis, *Christian Behaviour*, 44.

57. Ibid.

58. Ibid., 47–54.

59. The seventh and eighth talks broadcast November 1 and 8, 1942, respectively.

60. Lewis, *Christian Behaviour*, 54.

61. Ibid., 63.

62. Philippians 2:12.

63. Lewis, *Christian Behaviour*, 64.

CHAPTER 11

1. George Sayer, *Jack: C. S. Lewis and His Times* (New York: Harper and Row, 1988), 173.
2. Ibid.
3. Walter Hooper, interview with Justin Phillips, October 28, 1999, cited in Justin Phillips, *C. S. Lewis in a Time of War* (New York: HarperCollins, 2002), 222.
4. Sayer, *Jack: C. S. Lewis and His Times*, 174.
5. "Religion: Don v. Devil," *Time* 50, no. 10 (September 8, 1947).
6. Clyde S. Kilby and Marjorie Lamp Mead, eds., *Brothers and Friends* (New York: HarperCollins, 1982), 239–40.
7. C. S. Lewis, quoted by John Wain, "A Great Clerke," in James T. Como, ed., *C. S. Lewis at the Breakfast Table and Other Reminiscences* (New York: Macmillan, 1979), 69.
8. Letter from Eric Fenn to C. S. Lewis, March 10, 1943, quoted in Justin Phillips, *C. S. Lewis in a Time of War* (New York: HarperCollins, 2002), 224.
9. Letter from C. S. Lewis to Eric Fenn, March 13, 1943. See Phillips, *C. S. Lewis in a Time of War*, 224–5.
10. Letter from C. S. Lewis to Eric Fenn, April 12, 1943, in Hooper, *Collected Letters*, 2:568.
11. Letter from C. S. Lewis to Eric Fenn, May 7, 1943, in Hooper, *Collected Letters*, 2:571-2.
12. Letter from C. S. Lewis to Eric Fenn, June 16, 1943, in Hooper, *Collected Letters*, 2:581.
13. Letter from C. S. Lewis to Eric Fenn, July 1, 1943, in Hooper, *Collected Letters*, 2:582–3.
14. Letter from Eric Fenn to C. S. Lewis, July 21, 1943, quoted in Phillips, *C. S. Lewis in a Time of War*, 230-1.
15. The barrister was Nat Micklem. Phillips, *C. S. Lewis in a Time of War*, 232.
16. Ibid., 181.
17. Letter from C. S. Lewis to Sister Penelope, October 5, 1943. Hooper, *Collected Letters*, 2:592.

18. Ibid.

19. Letter from C. S. Lewis to Sister Penelope, October 21, 1944. Ibid., 2:628.

20. Letter from C. S. Lewis to Arthur Greeves, December 20, 1943. Ibid., 2:595.

21. Ibid., 2:596.

22. Internal memo from A. C. F. Beales to Eric Fenn, December 20, 1943. See Phillips, *C. S. Lewis in a Time of War*, 232.

23. Letter from Eric Fenn to C. S. Lewis, December 22, 1943. Hooper, *Collected Letters*, 2:597n.

24. Letter from C. S. Lewis to Eric Fenn, December 27, 1943. Hooper, *Collected Letters*, 2:598.

25. Letter from Eric Fenn to C. S. Lewis, December 29, 1943. Hooper, *Collected Letters*, 2:599n.

26. Letter from C. S. Lewis to Eric Fenn, January 9, 1944, in Hooper, *Collected Letters*, 2:601.

27. Letter from Eric Fenn to C. S. Lewis, February 10, 1944, in Hooper, *Collected Letters*, 2:602.

28. Ibid.

29. Ibid. It's worth noting that talks 2, 6, and 7 were recorded, but only talk 7, called "The New Man," has been found.

30. Ibid.

31. C. S. Lewis, *Beyond Personality: The Christian Idea of God* (London: Centenary Press, 1944), 9.

32. Ibid., 10.

33. "Making and Begetting," broadcast February 22, 1944. See Phillips, *C. S. Lewis in a Time of War*, 306.

34. Lewis, *Beyond Personality*, 14.

35. The second recorded talk was broadcast on February 29, 1944. See Phillips, *C. S. Lewis in a Time of War*, 306.

36. Lewis, *Beyond Personality*, 18.

37. Ibid.

38. Broadcast live on March 7, 1944. See Phillips, *C. S. Lewis in a Time of War*, 306.

39. Lewis, *Beyond Personality*, 28.

40. Ibid., 26.

41. Ibid., 28.

42. The fourth talk broadcast live on March 14, 1944. See Phillips, *C. S. Lewis in a Time of War*, 306.

43. Lewis, *Beyond Personality*, 32–33.

44. Broadcast live on March 21, 1944. See Phillips, *C. S. Lewis in a Time of War*, 306.

45. Lewis, *Beyond Personality*, 35–39.

46. The talk was recorded and then broadcast on March 28, 1944. See Phillips, *C. S. Lewis in a Time of War*, 306.

47. Lewis, *Beyond Personality*, 39–44.

48. Ibid., 44–57.

49. The talk was recorded and then broadcast on April 4, 1944. See Phillips, *C. S. Lewis in a Time of War*, 307.

50. Lewis, *Beyond Personality*, 61.

51. Ibid., 64.

52. *The Listener* 31, no. 789 (February 24, 1944); no. 790 (March 2, 1944); no. 791 (March 9, 1944); no. 792 (March 16, 1944); no. 793 (March 23, 1944); no. 794 (March 30, 1944); no. 795 (April 6, 1944).

53. Letter from C. S. Lewis to R. S. Lee, overseas religious broadcasting organizer, December 15, 1944, in Hooper, *Collected Letters*, 2:633.

54. Letter from J. W. Welch to C. S. Lewis, November 22, 1945. See Phillips, *C. S. Lewis in a Time of War*, 269.

55. M. Keith Booker, *The Chinua Achebe Encyclopedia* (Westport, CT: Greenwood Press, 2003), 275.

56. Chinua Achebe, interview by Jerome Brooks, quoted in "Chinua Achebe: The Art of Fiction No. 139," *Paris Review*, no. 133 (Winter 1994), http://www.theparisreview.org/interviews/1720/the-art-of-fiction-no-139-chinua-achebe.

57. Much of this information taken from the *Oxford Dictionary of National Biography*, Keith Clements, s.v. "Fenn, (John) Eric," accessed March 5, 2014, http://www.oxforddnb.com/view/printable/101335.

CHAPTER 12

1. "Republic/Ford JB-2 Loon (V-1 Buzz Bomb)," Fact Sheet, National Museum of the US Air Force, February 4, 2011, http://www.nationalmuseum.af.mil/factsheets/factsheet.asp?id=510.

2. "V-2 with Meillerwagen," Fact Sheet, National Museum of the US Air Force, February 4, 2011, http://www.nationalmuseum.af.mil/factsheets/factsheet.asp?id=511.

3. Humphrey Carpenter, ed., *The Letters of J. R. R. Tolkien* (London: Allen and Unwin, 1981), 71.

4. Walter Hooper, *C. S. Lewis: A Companion and Guide* (New York: HarperCollins, 1996), 281. See also C. S. Lewis, "Hell," in *The Problem of Pain* (London: Centenary Press, 1940), 106–116.

5. Letter from C. S. Lewis to Sister Penelope, September 6, 1944. Walter Hooper, ed., *The Collected Letters of C. S. Lewis,* vol. 2, *Books, Broadcasts, and the War, 1931–1949* (New York: HarperCollins, 2004), 624.

6. Letter from C. S. Lewis to Charles A. Brady, October 29, 1944. Ibid., 2:631.

7. Letter from C. S. Lewis to Mr. McClain, March 7, 1945. Ibid., 2:641.

8. Letter from C. S. Lewis to Dom Bede Griffiths, May 10, 1945. Ibid., 2:647–48.

9. Ibid., 2:648.

10. C. S. Lewis, ed. *Essays Presented to Charles Williams* (Grand Rapids: Eerdmans, 1966), xiii.

11. Ibid., xiv.

12. Clyde S. Kilby and Marjorie Lamp Mead, eds., *Brothers and Friends: The Diaries of Warren Hamilton Lewis* (New York: Harper and Row, 1982), 182–83.

13. Letter from C. S. Lewis to Owen Barfield, May 18, 1945. Hooper, *Collected Letters,* 2:651.

14. Walter Hooper, *C. S. Lewis: A Companion and Guide* (New York: HarperCollins, 1996), 239–40.

15. Kilby and Mead, *Brothers and Friends,* 196.

16. Hooper, *C. S. Lewis: A Companion and Guide*, 44.

17. Kilby and Mead, *Brothers and Friends*, 190.

18. Roger Lancelyn Green and Walter Hooper, *C. S. Lewis: A Biography* (London: Souvenir Press, 1988), 225–26.

19. Ibid., 225.

20. C. S. Lewis, *Of Other Worlds: Essays and Stories* (New York: Harcourt, 1994), 42.

21. Ibid.

22. Much has been said about Jack playing in a wardrobe as a child, with the assumption that this was the inspiration behind that first journey to Narnia. Doug Gresham, Jack's stepson, has stated adamantly in a note to the author that Jack loathed confined spaces and would never have willingly played inside a wardrobe.

23. Kilby and Mead, *Brothers and Friends*, 225–26.

24. George Sayer, *Jack: C. S. Lewis and His Times* (New York: Harper and Row, 1988), 199.

25. Letter from C. S. Lewis to Don Giovanni Calabria, January 14, 1949. Hooper, *Collected Letters*, 2:905–6.

26. Kilby and Mead, *Brothers and Friends*, 226.

27. Letter from C. S. Lewis to Owen Barfield, June 23, 1949. Hooper, *Collected Letters*, 2:945.

28. Joy Davidman, quoted in Lyle Dorsett, *And God Came In* (Peabody, MA: Hendrickson, 2009), 71.

29. Letter from C. S. Lewis to Arthur Greeves, February 5, 1950, in Walter Hooper, ed., *The Collected Letters of C. S. Lewis,* vol. 3, *Narnia, Cambridge, and Joy, 1950–1963* (New York: HarperCollins, 2007), 29.

30. Letter from C. S. Lewis to Sister Penelope, December 30, 1950. Ibid., 3:79.

31. Letter from C. S. Lewis to Warfield M. Firor, December 6, 1950. Ibid., 3:67.

32. Kilby and Mead, *Brothers and Friends*, 236.

33. Letter from C. S. Lewis to the Prime Minister's secretary, December 4, 1950. Hooper, *Collected Letters*, 3:147.

34. C. S. Lewis, *Mere Christianity* (London: Geoffrey Bles, 1952), vi.

35. Letter from C. S. Lewis to Nathan Comfort Starr, September 4, 1963. Hooper, *Collected Letters*, 3:1454.

36. Ibid.

37. Letter from C. S. Lewis to Arthur Greeves, September 11, 1963. Ibid. 3:1456.

38. W. H. Lewis, ed. "Memoir of C. S. Lewis," in *Letters of C. S. Lewis* (London: Geoffrey Bles, 1966), 24.

39. At approximately this same time, across the Atlantic Ocean, President John F. Kennedy was in a motorcade riding toward Dealey Plaza.

40. C. S. Lewis, "The World's Last Night," in *The World's Last Night and Other Essays* (Orlando, FL: Harcourt, 1988), 104–105.

41. Hooper, *Collected Letters*, 3:1457.

42. Paraphrase of Hamlet, in Shakespeare, *Hamlet*, act I, scene 2.

Bibliography

WORKS BY C.S. LEWIS
Lewis, C. S. *The Abolition of Man.* New York: Macmillan, 1947.
———. *Christian Reflections.* Edited by Walter Hooper. London:
Geoffrey Bles, 1967; Grand Rapids: Eerdmans, 1967.
———, ed. *George MacDonald: An Anthology.* London: Geoffrey Bles,
1946; New York: Macmillan, 1947.
———. *God in the Dock: Essays on Theology and Ethics.* Edited by
Walter Hooper. Grand Rapids: Eerdmans, 1970. Also published as
Undeceptions: Essays on Theology and Ethics. London: Geoffrey Bles,
1971.
———. *Mere Christianity.* London: Geoffrey Bles, 1952; New York:
Macmillan, 1952.
———. *The Problem of Pain.* London: Centenary Press, 1940.
———. *The Screwtape Letters.* London: Geoffrey Bles, 1942.
———. *Screwtape Proposes a Toast.* New York: HarperCollins, 1961.
———. *Surprised by Joy: The Shape of My Early Life.* New York:
Harcourt, Brace, 1956.
———. *The Weight of Glory, and Other Addresses.* Revised and
expanded. Edited by Walter Hooper. New York: Macmillan,
1980. Five of these essays originally appeared in C. S. Lewis,
Transposition, and Other Addresses (London: Geoffrey Bles,
1949) and *The Weight of Glory, and Other Addresses* (New York:
Macmillan, 1949).

COLLECTED LETTERS OF C.S. LEWIS
Hooper, Walter, ed. *The Collected Letters of C. S. Lewis.* Vol. 2, *Books,
Broadcasts, and the War (1931–1949).* New York: HarperCollins,
2004.
———. *The Collected Letters of C. S. Lewis.* Vol. 3, *Narnia, Cambridge,
and Joy (1950–1963).* New York: HarperCollins, 2007.
———. *They Stand Together: The Letters of C. S. Lewis to Arthur Greeves
(1914–1963).* New York: Macmillan, 1979.

Lewis, W. H., ed. *Letters of C. S. Lewis.* London: Geoffrey Bles, 1966.

ABOUT C. S. LEWIS AND THE INKLINGS

Carpenter, Humphrey, ed. *The Letters of J. R. R. Tolkien.* London: Allen and Unwin, 1981.

Como, James T., ed. *C. S. Lewis at the Breakfast Table and Other Reminiscences.* New York: Macmillan, 1979.

Dorsett, Lyle W. *And God Came In: The Extraordinary Story of Joy Davidman.* New York: Macmillan, 1983.

Duriez, Colin. *J. R. R. Tolkien and C. S. Lewis: The Story of Their Friendship.* Phoenix Mill, UK: Sutton, 2003.

Gibb, Jocelyn, ed. *Light on C. S. Lewis.* London: Geoffrey Bles, 1965.

Green, Roger Lancelyn, and Walter Hooper. *C. S. Lewis: A Biography.* London: Collins, 1974.

Hooper, Walter. *Through Joy and Beyond: A Pictorial Biography of C. S. Lewis.* New York: Macmillan, 1982.

———. *C. S. Lewis: A Companion and Guide.* New York: HarperCollins, 1996.

———. *C. S. Lewis: A Complete Guide to His Life and Works.* New York: HarperCollins, 1996.

Jacobs, Alan. *The Narnian: The Life and Imagination of C. S. Lewis.* New York: HarperCollins, 2005.

Kilby, Clyde S., and Marjorie Lamp Mead, eds. *Brothers and Friends: The Diaries of Major Warren Hamilton Lewis.* New York: Harper and Row, 1982.

Lindskoog, Kathryn. *C. S. Lewis: Mere Christian.* Wheaton, IL: Shaw, 1987.

Phillips, Justin. *C. S. Lewis at the BBC: Messages of Hope in the Darkness of War.* New York: HarperCollins, 2002.

———. *C. S. Lewis in a Time of War.* New York: HarperCollins, 2002.

Sayer, George. *Jack: C. S. Lewis and His Times.* New York: Harper and Row, 1988.

Sayers, Dorothy L. *The Man Born to Be King.* 2nd ed. Foreword by J. W. Welch. London: Victor Gollancz, 1957.

ABOUT THE BBC AND THE WORLD OF C. S. LEWIS

Braithwaite, Brian, Noelle Walsh, and Glyn Davies, comps. *The Home Front: The Best of Good Housekeeping (1939–1945)*. London: Leopard Books, 1987.

Briggs, Asa. *The BBC: The First Fifty Years*. Oxford: Oxford University Press, 1985.

Briggs, Susan. *Keep Smiling Through*. London: Weidenfeld and Nicolson, 1975.

The British People at War. London: Odhams, 1944.

Collier, Richard. *1940: The World in Flames*. London: Hamish Hamilton, 1979.

Deedes, William F. *A.R.P.: A Complete Guide to Civil Defence Measures*. London: *Daily Telegraph*, 1939.

Front Line, 1940–41: The Official Story of the Civil Defence of Britain. London: H. M. Stationery Office, 1942.

Gibbon, Constantine Fitz. *The Blitz*. London: Wingate, 1957.

Green, Benny. *Britain at War*. Godalming, UK: Coombe Books, 1993.

Harrisson, Tom. *Living Through the Blitz: Witnesses to War*. New York: Schocken Books, 1989.

Hickman, Tom. *What Did You Do in the War, Auntie?: The BBC at War, 1939–1945*. London: BBC Books, 1995.

Hill, Maureen. *Britain at War: Unseen Archives*. Bath, UK: Parragon Book Service, 2002.

Longmate, Norman. *How We Lived Then: A History of Everyday Life During the Second World War*. London: Arrow Books, 1973.

Lynn, Vera. *We'll Meet Again: A Personal and Social History of World War Two*. London: Sidgwick and Jackson, 1994.

Minns, Raynes. *Bombers and Mash: The Domestic Front, 1939–45*. London: Virago, 1980.

Murrow, Edward R. *This Is London*. Witnesses to War, edited by Elmer Davis. New York: Simon and Schuster, 1941.

Opie, Robert, comp. *The Wartime Scrapbook: From Blitz to Victory (1939–1945)*. London: New Cavendish Books, 1995.

Ramsey, Winston G., ed. *The Blitz: Then and Now*. Vol. 2. London: Battle of Britain Prints, 1988.

Ray, John. *The Night Blitz (1940–1941)*. London: Cassell, 1996.

Shirer, William L. *The Rise and Fall of the Third Reich: A History of Nazi Germany*. New York: Simon and Schuster, 1960.

Wicks, Ben. *Waiting for the All Clear: True Stories from Survivors of the Blitz*. London: Bloomsbury, 1990.

Ziegler, Philip. *London at War (1939–1945)*. New York: Knopf, 1995.

FOCUS ON THE FAMILY®

Welcome to the Family

Whether you purchased this book, borrowed it, or received it as a gift, thanks for reading it! This is just one of many insightful, biblically based resources that Focus on the Family produces for people in all stages of life.

Focus is a global Christian ministry dedicated to helping families thrive as they celebrate and cultivate God's design for marriage and experience the adventure of parenthood. Our outreach exists to support individuals and families in the joys and challenges they face, and to equip and empower them to be the best they can be.

Through our many media outlets, we offer help and hope, promote moral values and share the life-changing message of Jesus Christ with people around the world.

Focus on the Family MAGAZINES

These faith-building, character-developing publications address the interests, issues, concerns, and challenges faced by every member of your family from preschool through the senior years.

For More INFORMATION

 ONLINE:
Log on to
FocusOnTheFamily.com
In Canada, log on to
FocusOnTheFamily.ca

 PHONE:
Call toll-free:
**800-A-FAMILY
(232-6459)**
In Canada, call toll-free:
800-661-9800

THRIVING FAMILY®	FOCUS ON	FOCUS ON	FOCUS ON
Marriage & Parenting	THE FAMILY CLUBHOUSE JR.® Ages 4 to 8	THE FAMILY CLUBHOUSE® Ages 8 to 12	THE FAMILY CITIZEN® U.S. news issues

Rev. 3/11

Meet the rest of the family

**Expert advice on parenting and marriage . . .
spiritual growth . . . powerful personal stories . . .**

Focus on the Family's collection of inspiring, practical resources can help your family grow closer to God—and each other—than ever before. Whichever format you need—video, audio, book or eBook—we have something for you. Visit our online Family Store and discover how we can help your family thrive at **FocusOnTheFamily.com/resources.**